STO

4-21-75

Lecture Notes in Economics and Mathematical Systems

Managing Editors: M. Beckmann and H. P. Künzi

Mathematical Economics

104

Shozaburo Fujino

A Neo-Keynesian Theory of Inflation and Economic Growth

Springer-Verlag
Berlin · Heidelberg · New York 1974

Library of Congress Cataloging in Publication Data

Fujino, Shozaburo, 1927-
    A neo-Keynesian theory of inflation and economic
growth.

    (Lecture notes in economics and mathematical systems,
104. Mathematical economics)
    Bibliography: p.
    1. Inflation (Finance) 2. Saving and investment.
3. Economic development. 4. Money. I. Title.
II. Series: Lecture notes in economics and mathematical systems, 104. III. Series: Mathematical economics.
HG229.F84   332.4'1   74-19273

AMS Subject Classifications (1970): 90 A 99

ISBN 3-540-06964-X Springer-Verlag Berlin · Heidelberg · New York
ISBN 0-387-06964-X Springer-Verlag New York · Heidelberg · Berlin

Offsetprinting and bookbinding: Julius Beltz, Hemsbach/Bergstr.

CONTENTS

Acknowledgements

Numerous people have given comments on papers included in this note. However, the author would particularly like to thank M. Abramovitz, M. Beckmann, D. K. Foley, S. Koizumi, R. I. Mackinnon, K. Obi, R. Sato, E. S. Shaw, J. L. Stein, and G. S. Suzawa. In addition, he is grateful to G. S. Suzawa and E. Maciejewski for correcting and improving the English content of his original manuscript, and to Mrs. H. Fujisawa for expert typing.

Tokyo, July 1974

Shozaburo Fujino

GENERAL INTRODUCTION

The purposes of this study are to investigate processes of cyclical fluctuations, inflation and economic growth, and concomitantly, to relate the short-run analysis to the long-run analysis of the economy as far as feasible under the confines of this investigation.

First of all, we shall present a theory of investment in Chapter 1. We shall make evident defects included in the neo-classical theory of investment, founded in particular by I. Fisher and a variant of which is the Keynesian version, by taking into account recent studies of investment and by formulating a new theory of investment. Its incorporation into our dynamic analyses is one of the reasons why the theory developed in this study is referred to as Neo-Keynesian. Briefly, the theory is characterized by firm investment being a function of the firm's expected stock of money, the expected marginal productivity of capital, and the expected rate of inflation (or the firm's subjective rate of real interest).

Secondly, depending on our analysis of investment in Chapter 1, we shall proceed in our examinations of cyclical growth, inflation and monetary growth in Chapters 2, through 5. In Chapter 2 we shall, first of all, formulate our basic relationships with respect to saving-investment and to the demand for and supply of money. In this instance we shall distinguish between the short-run and long-run phases of these relationships, the former of which would be valid for explaining cyclical growth and inflation, and the latter of which for examining the long-run tendencies of economic variables in monetary growth.

On analyzing cyclical growth, inflation and monetary growth, we shall assume three patterns with respect to the flexibility of wage rates: we shall assume that the rate of money wage is rigid in analyzing cyclical growth, that it restores flexibility in the case of inflation, and that the rate of real wage becomes flexible in the process of monetary growth where we might take, say, ten years as our unit-period to analyze long-term tendencies of economic variables. Thus, considering that we postulate flexible nominal wage rate and flexible real wage rate as well as rigid nominal wage, there is added reason to describe our theory as "Neo-Keynesian".

In Chapter 3 we shall conceive of business cycles not as cyclical fluctuations of the absolute level, say of output, but rather as cyclical fluctuations in the rate of growth, since in economies experiencing rapid growth, e.g. the Japanese economy, there do not appear to be cyclical fluctuations in the absolute levels of economic variables. This treatment of fluctuations enables us to directly relate our analysis of business cycles to that of economic growth. We shall show in this chapter that our short-run basic relationships will produce, with help of some additional assumptions, a model of growth cycle which, formally speaking, has the same non-linear characteristics with regards to its saving-investment relationship as the famous Kaldor model of business cycles, although our model is derived from different considerations.

In Chapter 4, a dynamic theory of inflation will be developed. It seems that recent inflation experienced in advanced economies is closely related to changes in the market structure which take place in connection with full employment policies, because those policies make it easier for firms to realize their requests with respect to prices and at the same time induce wage rate flexibility. We shall call a sustained increase in the price level caused by the transition of money wage rate from rigidity to flexibility as employment inflation, which we will illustrate by means of a kind of short-run growth model. It will be shown that this analysis is able to explain the so-called stagflation.

In Chapter 5 we shall construct a model of monetary growth by taking into account our long-run basic relationships to explain secular tendencies of the labor productivity, the capital-labor ratio, the output-capital ratio, the real money-capital ratio and so forth. In particular we shall endeavor to explain the rising tendency of the real money-capital ratio over time, which is empirically observed, by the steady state growth features of our model, although the ratio remains constant in the steady state of the usual analysis of monetary growth.

CHAPTER 1

A THEORY OF INVESTMENT

1. 1 Problems in the Neo-classical Theory of Investment

According to the Keynesian theory of investment, the firm determines the optimal amount of investment by taking into consideration the marginal efficiency of capital and the rate of interest. In order words, it asserts that the firm determines investment so as to equate the demand price to the market price of capital goods.[1] This investment behavior implies that a firm determines its optimal stock of capital by maximizing its present value with respect to its capital stock and labor input.[2] That is, the Keynesian theory of investment is

---

1) On defining the marginal efficiency of capital, Keynes employs the supply price instead of the market price of capital goods. Apart from the case where the investing firm behaves monopsonically in the market of capital goods, we might suppose, however, that it would behave under a given price of capital goods. Then we should be concerned with not the supply price but the market price of capital goods. See J. M. Keynes: The General Theory of Employment, Interest and Money, 1936, p. 135.

2) Suppose that the duration period of capital stock is T and that production function is given by

   (1) $Y_r(t) = F[K, N(t)]$, $t\varepsilon(0, T)$.

   Then the firm's prospective revenue from selling output produced by K at t less operating expenses is given by $[p(t)Y_r(t) - w(t)N(t)]$, where $p(t)$ denotes the firm's expected price of the output at t and $w(t)$ the expected rate of wage at t. Let us define the present value of the firm by

   (2) $\Pi \equiv \int_0^T [p(t)Y_r(t) - w(t)N(t)] e^{-it} dt - p_K K$,

   where i is the rate of interest and p_K the market price of capital goods. If we postulate that the firm will determine K and N(t) so that Π can be maximized, then we can get from the first order condition of a maximum

   (3) $\int_0^T p(t) \dfrac{\partial Y_r(t)}{\partial K} e^{-it} dt = p_K$,

   and

   (4) $p(t) \dfrac{\partial Y_r(t)}{\partial N(t)} = w(t)$.

On the other hand, if the firm initially employs capital stock K_0 and labor N_0, then

(5) $K = K_0 + I_r$,

and

(6) $N(t) = N_0 + \Delta N(t)$,

where I_r is real investment and $\Delta N(t)$ is the increase of labor input at t compared with that at the initial point of time. Therefore the production function will be expressed as follows;

(7) $Y_r(t) = F[K_0 + I_r, N_0 + \Delta(t)]$.

In addition let us define

(8) $\Delta Y_r(t) \equiv Y_r(t) - Y_{r_0}$,

where $Y_{r_0} = F[K_0, N_0]$.

Now, denote the prospective yield per unit of capital goods brought about by real investment I_r at t by $R(t)$. Then we obtain

(9) $R(t) = \dfrac{1}{I_r} [p(t)\Delta Y_r(t) - w(t)\Delta N(t)]$.

Therefore, the marginal efficiency of capital r will be given by

(10) $p_K = \int_0^T [R(t)/I_r] e^{-rt} \, dt$.

At the same time, the demand price of capital goods p_K^D is obtained by

(11) $p_K^D = \int_0^T [R(t)/I_r] e^{-it} \, dt$.

When I_r approaches zero infinitely under the condition of $\Delta N(t) = 0$ in equations (10) and (11), we obtain

(12) $p_K = \int_0^T p(t) \dfrac{\partial Y_r(t)}{\partial K} e^{-rt} \, dt$,

and

(13) $p_K^D = \int_0^T p(t) \dfrac{\partial Y_r(t)}{\partial K} e^{-it} \, dt$.

nothing more than the neo-classical theory of firm's behavior.

The neo-classical theory of investment, however, contains various problems. First of all, it cannot explain the existence of permanently positive investment. After actual capital stock has been adjusted to the optimal stock of capital, investment should be zero, if there is no change in any of the conditions which were given on the firm's planning of the optimal stock of capital, i.e., the expected price of output, the expected rate of wage, the price of capital goods, the rate of interest, and so on. Except in a few years when business activities are abnormally sluggish, actual investment is positive year after year. How then does the neo-classical theory explain the continuing positive investment ? This question was raised by T. Haavelmo. The neo-classical theory provides, he thinks, no sufficient answer for the growth of optimal capital stock itself.[3]

One answer to that question, which is immediately apparent, is the existence of continuous changes in the production function brought on by a series of technological advances. But Haavelmo believes that this could result not only in positive but also negative investment. Secondly, there is the possibility that continuous positive investment prevails if the price of capital goods falls continuously, or if the rate of change of the rate of interest were always negative, or if the expected price of output or the expected rate of wage were always rising.[4]

Therefore, when p_K is equal to p_K^D, we get

(14) $\quad p_K = \int_0^T p(t) \, \dfrac{\partial Y_r(t)}{\partial K} \, e^{-it} \, dt.$

Equation (14) is nothing but equation (3).

3) T. Haavelmo: A Study in the Theory of Investment, 1960, pp. 162-165.

4) T. Haavelmo: op. cit., pp. 170-172.

D. W. Jorgenson attempts to explain investment behavior as the movement of the rate of change of the optimal stock of capital within the framework of the neo-classical theory by supposing continuous changes of various prices over time.[5] But it seems doubtful that the existence of annually positive investment can be explained by the changes of various prices. Rather, if there could exist a factor within the framework of the neo-classical theory which accounts for the rate of growth of the optimal stock of capital to be positive, then it must be the continuous progress of technology. Even without adopting the neo-classical approach, this would appear to be the most plausible explanation of the existence of permanently positive investment. For example, if we supposed that labor-augmenting technical progress occurs continuously, the marginal productivity of capital would tend to increase so that the schedule of marginal efficiency of capital would shift rightward successively. As a result, investment would be always positive, although there were no change in the equilibrium marginal productivity of capital or the equilibrium marginal efficiency of capital observed under a given rate of interest.

A second problem in the neo-classical theory of investment arises when we attempt to relate it with the capital stock adjustment principle.[6] It eminates from the fact that the capital stock adjustment process is not directly derived from the optimizing behavior of the firm. This is also pointed out by Haavelmo.[7]

In regard to this second problem, R. Eisner and R. H. Strotz have attempted to derive an explanation of investment behavior itself from the firm's optimizing behavior. That is, assuming that the firm incurs costs on its investment activities, they derive investment behavior from the firm's present value maximizing

---

5) D. W. Jorgenson: The Theory of Investment Behavior, Determinants of Investment Behavior, edited by R. Ferber, 1967, pp. 129-155.

6) Regarding the capital stock adjustment principle, see R. C. O. Matthews: The Trade Cycle, 1959, pp. 40-43.

7) T. Haavelmo: op. cit., pp. 172-174.

behavior taking into account the adjustment costs.[8] And the study in this direction is deepened by R. E. Lucas, Jr., J. P. Gould, A. B. Treadway and so forth.[9] The reasons why a firm should have expenses over expenditures for the capital goods themselves are given in these studies as follows: the firm consists of both a production sector and a planning sector, thereby paying costs for activities in the planning sector as well, and furthermore when new capital goods are set up, they are operated effectively only after some learning period since frequently a new technique is adopted.[10]

Especially in their studies, Eisner and Strotz, Lucas, and Gould, make it clear that the capital stock adjustment function itself can be derived from the firm's optimizing behavior, taking into consideration adjustment costs, even if the production function is linear homogeneous. Thus to some extent they deal not only with the second problem but also a third one.[11]

The third problem arises when we suppose a linear homogeneous production function. For, as is well known, we are unable to determine the scale of the optimal stock of capital, although we can determine the optimal degree of capital intensity by the firm's present value maximizing behavior.

A forth problem of the neo-classical theory centers particularly on the firm's capital stock and money balances and does not refer to the firm's demand

8) R. Eisner & R. H. Strotz: Determinants of Business Investments, Commission on Money and Credit, Impacts of Monetary Policy, 1963, pp. 59-337.

9) R. E. Lucas, Jr. : Optimal Investment Policy and the Flexible Acceterator, International Economic Review, Vol. 8, Feb. 1967, pp. 78-85. R. E. Lucas, Jr. : Adjustment Costs and the Theory of Supply, Journal of Political Economy, Vol. 75, Aug. 1967, Part I, pp. 321-334. J. P. Gould: Adjustment Costs in the Theory of Investment of the Firm, Review of Economic Studies, Vol. 35, Jan. 1968, pp. 47-55. A. B. Treadway: On Rational Entrepreneurial Behavior and the Demand for Investment, Review of Economic Studies, Vol. 36, April. 1969, pp. 228-239.

10) R. E. Lucas, Jr. : Adjustment Costs and the Theory of Supply, op. cit., p. 324.

11) In his "Optimal Investment Policy", Lucas assumes that production function is linear homogeneous in regard to capital and labor, but he supposes in his "Adjustment Costs" that production function includes costs in investment activities and it is linear homogeneous with respect to capital, labor, and gross investment.

for other assets. The firm holds money balance as well as physical capital stock, if we suppose the simplest case. The neo-classical theory fails to satisfactorily explain the firm's simultaneous holdings of capital stock and money balance. A comprehensive theory has to explain the holdings of capital stock and money balance and in addition the firm's demand for loanable funds to finance these holdings.

And finally the neo-classical theory is not concerned with "uncertainty in transactions". Uncertainty in transactions could occur even under perfect competition. And it is of importance in the firm's long run planning. It might be suitable, in analyzing the firm's behavior, to suppose that the adjustment costs introduced by Eisner, Strotz and so on are the result of extra expenses to expand the firm's selling network, by which it hopes to avoid uncertainty about the future sales of investment good outputs rather than costs relating to planning and learning.

In the following analysis we shall attach importance to the continuous occurrence of technical progress to explain the existence of permanently positive investment.

Regarding the second problem of the neo-classical theory, it seems that the method adopted by Eisner-Strotz and so forth is certainly one of possible approaches to understanding rationale firm behavior. But the restraint complex surrounding the firm is very complicated and its content may change depending on the length of the period under consideration. Generally speaking, the longer the unit period for analysis, the more the conditions will cease to be constraints on the firm. If firms in the real world were restricted by such constraints, they will incur some additional costs or suffer some form of burden when they operate in the face of all these constraints. It may be possible that the costs do not bring forth the benefits necessary to compensate for them. Under the circumstance the firm would rather plan the optimal stock of capital with respect to the long-run period, where the number of constraints would be comparatively few, and temporarily it would resort to the practice of a simple rule of thumb of the sort on which the capital stock adjustment principle is based. We shall adopt this point of view, although we will examine rational firm behavior in our future study.

We shall endeavor in the following analysis to solve the third, fourth and fifth problems of the neo-classical theory.

1. 2   Firm's Investment Function and Its Demand For Money Function

We assume that the firm we are concerned with holds capital stock and money balance as its assets, issues securities to finance their holdings, and produces output by using capital and labor. In addition, we assume that the firm acts under perfect competition in all markets, where uncertainty exists. The transactions which are taken into consideration with respect to the firm's investing activities regarding capital are as follows: (1) sales of output produced in the future as the result of capital formation, (2) purchases of labor in the future for use in conjunction with capital, (3) present purchases of capital goods, and (4) present acquisition of money balance (or funds).

Uncertainty on transactions will be larger in the case of sales of output to obtain money balance than in the case of exchange of money for goods, for as J. Hirshleifer points out, money is a social contrivance for minimizing the cost of reducing uncertainty on transactions,[12] and related to this point is the fact that money is the most liquid relative to other goods. Therefore, we will ignore uncertainty on transactions in (2) purchases of labor and (3) purchases of capital goods. Although there will exist uncertainty on transactions in purchasing labor, especially in the neighborhood of full employment, we shall ignore it in the following analysis.[13], [14] Thus, uncertainty on transactions should matter

---

12) J. Hirshleifer: Investment, Interest and Capital, 1970. p. 243.

13) Alternatively, we may suppose that labor input (or capital input) is required to obtain labor, and the former is included in labor input (or capital input) as a whole.

14) In the usual analysis of portfolio-selection, uncertainty on transactions is neglected. The reason why we may suppose so is that the objectives there deal mainly with financial assets, so that liquidity is implicitly assumed to be high.

in the cases of (1) sales of output and (2) acquisition of money balance or funds.
In the short run, anticipated sales will be a random-variable with a finite mean,
which is independent of anticipated price, because of uncertainty on transactions.
And the firm will, we may suppose, behave on the basis of the mathematical expectation of a utility function to be defined later. In the long run, where we are
concerned with accumulating capital goods, however, the firm could overcome uncertainty on sales of output by means of establishing a network or an organization
for sales and/or supplying informations about products of the firm through adver-
tisements. Therefore, we shall suppose that capital and labor are used to form
the sales organization, and that they are included with the capital and the labor
inputs that enter the production function. Thus we have to conceive of output as
a result not only of the physical activities of production but also of sales activities. Let us denote real output by Y_r and assume that it is a linear homogeneous function of capital stock K and labor input N. Namely

(1. 1) $Y_r = F(K, N)$.

We shall assume that the amount of money balance acquired by the firm is a given
random-variable with a finite mean, because the firm will be concerned with it at
the time of planning of capital investment. Let us denote the firm's real money
balance by ($\overline{M}/P$), where P is the general price level and $\overline{M}$ is a random variable.

Next let us suppose that the firm's utility is an increasing function of the
present value of stream of real prospective yields obtained by capital investment
and real money balance, respectively, and a decreasing function of the real supply
of securities. The firm plans, we shall assume, its holdings of assets so that
it will maximize its expected utility. Denote the present value of stream of
prospective yields by $\overline{R}$, the supply of securities by B_S. Then, the firm's utility
function is represented

(1. 2) $\overline{U} = \overline{U}(\dfrac{\overline{R}}{P}, \dfrac{\overline{M}}{P}, -\dfrac{B_S}{P})$, $\overline{U}_1 > 0$, $\overline{U}_2 > 0$, $\overline{U}_3 > 0$.[15)]

Stock variables of the firm should satisfy the following constraint of balance-sheet;

(1. 3) $p_K K + \overline{M} = B_S$,

where p_K is the price of capital goods. Thus, if $\overline{U}$ is a homogeneous function of zero degree in regard to $(\overline{R}/P)$, $(\overline{M}/P)$, and $(-B_S/P)$, then we obtain

(1. 4) $\overline{U} = \overline{U} \left[\dfrac{\overline{R}}{p_K K}, \dfrac{\overline{M}}{p_K K}, - \left(1 + \dfrac{\overline{M}}{p_K K} \right) \right].$

There is no change in the following analysis, if we express $\overline{M}$ by B_S instead of representing B_S by $\overline{M}$. B_S will then be the random variable. The reason why we use $\overline{M}$ here is this: the variable which affects the mathematical expectation of $\overline{M}$ or B_S is ultimately the supply of money M_S, to which $\overline{M}$ rather than B_S seems to be more appropriate.

Now, is the rate of interest, by which the firm plans investment, the market rate ? It seems that a firm takes into account its own implicit rate of interest which it deems to be adequate. The difference between this subjective rate of interest and the market rate depends on the degree of risk bound up with the investment.[16]   Denote the subjective rate of interest by θ, the duration period of capital goods by T, the anticipated price of products at t by $\overline{p}_e(t)$, and the anticipated rate of wage at t by $\overline{w}_e(t)$. Then $\overline{R}$ can be expressed as follows:

(1. 5) $\overline{R} = \int_0^T \left[\overline{p}_e(t) Y_r(t) - \overline{w}_e(t) N(t) \right] e^{-\theta t} \, dt.$

---

15) We might suppose that the firm's utility is a function of the present value of the firm rather than $(\overline{R}/P)$. And if the former were expressed by $[(\overline{R} - B_S)/P]$ because the firm not only invested capital stock but also held money balance, then $\overline{U}$ would be an increasing function of $[(\overline{R} - B_S)/P]$. But, then $\overline{U}$ is an increasing function of $(\overline{R}/P)$ and a decreasing function of (B_S/P). And at the same time $\overline{U}$ is a decreasing function of (B_S/P) by other reason than it is a function of the present value of the firm. Therefore summing up these two effects of $\overline{B}_S/P$ on $\overline{U}$, we suppose that $\overline{U}$ is an increasing function of $(\overline{R}/P)$ and a decreasing function of (B_S/P) as shown in the text.

16) E. Schneider: Einführung in die Wirtschaftstheorie, II. Teil, 1960, pp. 233-234.

We shall assume that $\bar{p}_e(t)$ changes at an expected rate of inflation $\bar{\pi}_e$, so that it is expressed by $pe^{\bar{\pi}_e t}$, where p is the price of products at the present, and $\bar{\pi}_e$ is a random variable. We assume also that the anticipated real rate of wage ($\bar{w}_e$ $(t)/\bar{p}_e(t)$) is a constant and equals the expected marginal productivity of labor under the degree of capital intensity at the time of planning. We get then

$$(1.\ 6) \quad \bar{R} = \int_0^T p\ [Y_r(t) - F_N^e(k_0)N(t)]\ e^{-(\theta - \bar{\pi}_e)t}\ dt,$$

where $F_N^e(k_0)$ is the expected marginal productivity of labor under the degree of capital intensity at the time of planning, k_0, and $(\theta - \bar{\pi}_e)$ is the subjective real rate of interest. Since relationships among $\bar{p}_e$, $\bar{w}_e$, and $\bar{\pi}_e$, are fixed within the duration period of capital goods, K and N used at each point of time are same, so that Y_r is constant in the period. When we suppose that T is sufficiently large, we can obtain

$$(1.\ 7) \quad \bar{R} = p[Y_r - F_N^e(k_0)N]\ \frac{1}{\theta - \bar{\pi}_e}.$$

Denote the expected value of $[1/(\theta - \bar{\pi}_e)]$ by $[1/(\theta - \pi_e)]$, then

$$(1.\ 8) \quad E[\ \bar{R}\ ] \equiv R = p[Y_r - F_N^e(k_0)N]\ \frac{1}{\theta - \pi_e},$$

where, of course, π_e is not always equal to the expected value of $\bar{\pi}_e$. But we shall call π_e the expected rate of inflation in the following. Let us express the standard deviation of $\bar{R}$ by σ_R, that of $[1/(\theta - \bar{\pi}_e)]$ by σ_δ, and the mean of $[1/(\theta - \bar{\pi}_e)]$ by δ, then we get

$$(1.\ 9) \quad \sigma_R^2 = E[(\bar{R} - R)^2] = p^2[Y_r - F_N^e(k_0)]^2\ \sigma_\delta^2,$$

so that

$$(1.\ 10) \quad \frac{\sigma_R}{R} = \frac{\sigma_\delta}{\delta}.$$

13

That is, the coefficient of variation of $\bar{R}$ is equal to that of $[1/(\theta - \bar{\pi}_e)]$. Because (σ_δ/δ) is a constant, (σ_R/R), which we shall denote by v_R, is also a constant.

Now we shall assume that the expected value of the utility function (1. 4) is expressed as follows;

$$(1.\ 11) \quad E[\ \bar{U}\ ] = U^*[\ \frac{R}{p_K K},\ \frac{M}{p_K K},\ -(1 + \frac{M}{p_K K}),\ \frac{\sigma_R}{p_K K},\ \frac{\sigma_M}{p_K K}\ ],$$

where M is the expected value of $\bar{M}$, and σ_M is the standard deviation of $\bar{M}$. Denote (σ_M/M) by v_M. Then

$$(1.\ 12) \quad E[\ \bar{U}\ ] = U^*[\ \frac{R}{p_K K},\ \frac{M}{p_K K},\ -(1 + \frac{M}{p_K K}),\ v_R \frac{R}{p_K K},\ v_M \frac{M}{p_K K}\ ].$$

Since v_R and v_M are constant, we can express equation (1. 12) as follows;

$$(1.\ 13) \quad E[\ \bar{U}\ ] \equiv U = U[\ \frac{R}{p_K K},\ \frac{M}{p_K K},\ -(1 + \frac{M}{p_K K})\ ],$$

where we assume

$$(1.\ 14) \quad U_i > 0, \quad i = 1, 2, 3,$$

and

$$(1.\ 15) \quad U_{11} < 0.$$

In addition we suppose that $(U_2 - U_3)$, i.e., the expected marginal utility of $(M/p_K K)$ as a whole is decreasing. Namely,

$$(1.\ 16) \quad U_{22} - 2U_{23} + U_{33} < 0.$$

Furthermore $(U_2 - U_3)$ is, we shall assume, a decreasing function of $(R/p_K K)$. That is,

(1. 17) $U_{12} - U_{13} < 0.$

The first order conditions for a maximum of U with respect to K and N are

(1. 18) $\dfrac{\partial U}{\partial K} = U_1 \dfrac{pF_K K - p[\, Y_r - F_N^e(k_0)N \,]}{p_K K^2} \cdot \dfrac{1}{\theta - \pi_e} - U_2 \dfrac{M}{p_K K} + U_3 \dfrac{M}{p_K K^2} = 0,$

and

(1. 19) $\dfrac{\partial U}{\partial N} = U_1 \dfrac{p[\, F_N - F_N^e(k_0) \,]}{p_K K} \dfrac{1}{\theta - \pi_e} = 0.$

From equation (1. 19) we get

(1. 20) $F_N = F_N^e(k_0).$

Because the production function is linear homogeneous, we obtain

(1. 21) $Y_r = F_K K + F_N N.$

Therefore

(1. 22) $Y_r = F_K K + F_N^e(k_0)N,$

where F_K should be equal to $F_K^e(k_0)$.

Substituting equation (1. 22) into equation (1. 18), we get

(1. 23) $U_2 = U_3.$

At the same time from equations (1. 8) and (1. 22) we obtain

(1. 24) $\dfrac{R}{p_K K} = \dfrac{p}{p_K} F_K^e(k_0) \dfrac{1}{\theta - \pi_e}.$

Now, U_2 and U_3 are functions of $(R/p_K K)$ and $(M/p_K K)$, respectively, so that we get from equations (1. 23) and (1. 24)

$$(1.\ 25) \qquad \frac{M}{p_K K} = g[\ \frac{p}{p_K}\ F_K^e(k_0)\ \frac{1}{\theta - \pi_e}\ ],$$

where M, p, p_K, k_0, θ and π_e are given, so that the value of K is determined by equation (1. 25). We may refer to the g function in equation (1. 25) as the firm's demand for money function. That is, the ratio of the firm's demand for real money to capital stock is a function of the value of expected marginal productivity of capital capitalized by the subjective real rate of interest per unit value of capital goods. From equation (1. 23) we can get

$$(1.\ 26) \qquad \frac{d(\ \dfrac{M}{p_K K}\ )}{d(\ \dfrac{R}{p_K K}\ )} = - \frac{U_{12} - U_{13}}{U_{22} - 2U_{23} + U_{33}}.$$

Since $(U_{12} - U_{13}) < 0$ and $(U_{22} - 2U_{23} + U_{33}) < 0$, $(M/p_K K)$ should be a decreasing function of $(R/p_K K)$. Namely, g' should be negative. We might assume that $(M/p_K K)$ is zero when $(R/p_K K)$ is infinite.

The second order condition for a maximum is

$$(1.\ 27) \qquad U_{KK} < 0,\ U_{NN} < 0,\ \begin{vmatrix} U_{KK} & U_{KN} \\ U_{KN} & U_{NN} \end{vmatrix} > 0,$$

where

$$U_{KK} = U_1 \frac{pF_{KK}}{p_K K} \cdot \frac{1}{\theta - \pi_e} + (U_{22} - 2U_{23} + U_{33})(\ \frac{M}{p_K K^2}\ )^2,$$

$$(1.\ 28) \qquad U_{KN} = U_1 \frac{pF_{KK}}{p_K K} \cdot \frac{1}{\theta - \pi_e},$$

$$U_{NN} = U_1 \frac{pF_{NN}}{p_K K} \cdot \frac{1}{\theta - \pi_e}.$$

Because $F_{KK} < 0$ and $(U_{22} - 2U_{23} + U_{33}) < 0$, U_{KK} should be negative. At the same time, since $F_{NN} < 0$, U_{NN} should be negative. Because of the linear homogeneity of the production function

$$F_{KK} = - F_{KN} \frac{K}{N},$$

(1. 29)

$$F_{NN} = - F_{KN} \frac{K}{N}.$$

Thus, when taking into account equations (1. 28) and (1. 29), we get

(1. 30)
$$\begin{vmatrix} U_{KK} & U_{KN} \\ U_{KN} & U_{NN} \end{vmatrix} = U_1 \left(\frac{pF_{NN}}{p_K K^2} \right)^2 (U_{22} - 2U_{23} + U_{33}) \frac{1}{\theta - \pi_e} > 0.$$

Therefore, the second order condition for a maximum (1. 27) is satisfied under our assumptions.

As already shown above, the optimal capital stock of the firm will be determined so as to satisfy equation (1. 25). Let us denote it by K^*. The first factor to account for permanently positive investment is technical progress by which K^* is increased permanently. That is, if labor augmenting technical progress occurs continuously, there will be permanent increases in the marginal productivity of capital. Thus g will decrease, so that K^* will have to increase under a given M. In the following analysis we shall assume such a situation. Furthermore, if the expected rate of inflation π_e increases, K^* will be expanded. However the change in π_e will be a factor which leads to cyclical fluctuations in the rate of growth of K^* rather than to a permanent steady growth of K^*.

Thus we arrive at our investment function

$$(1.\ 31) \quad I_r = \alpha[\ K^* - K\ ] = \alpha[\ \frac{M}{gp_K} - K\ ], \quad 0 < \alpha < 1,$$

by which permanently positive investment can be explained. When the firm's optimal stock of capital and its demand for real money are determined as shown above,
the firm's optimal supply of real securities will be determined as the sum of both
these values. And the current supply of real securities will be equal to the sum
of the actual stock of capital and the demand for real money.

If there is only one commodity in the economy, which is permanently durable
when it is used as capital, then the product price of the firm p coincides with
the price of capital goods p_K and with the general price level P. Therefore the
firm's demand function for money will be given by

$$(1.\ 32) \quad \frac{M_D^f}{p_K K} = g[\ \frac{F_K^e(k\ )}{\theta - \pi_e}\ ].$$

In brief, the economic meaning of the above analysis is as follows. When the
firm designs its long run plan, there exists uncertainty on transactions to get
loanable funds, so that the firm's money balance or amount of funds obtained is
a random variable. Thus long run optimality is achieved under the circumstances
by including in the balance-sheet a mathematically expected fixed value of money
balance or amount of funds obtained. As a result, the optimal stock of capital
of the firm will have to be such that the firm's optimal balance of money will be
equal to that expected to inflow into the firm. That is, the firm's optimal a-
mount of funds will be equilibrated to the expected inflow of funds. The appli-
cability of our investment function thus derived is not confined to the situation
with credit-rationing. As far as there exists uncertainty with respect to obtain-
ing money balance, whether or not banks practice credit-rationing, the function

is useful in explaining the behavior of investment.[17]

Finally, one last point should be made regarding the above analysis. It refers to the demand for labor. According to the above analysis, the demand for labor is formally determined as a function of the expected rate of real wage and the optimal stock of capital. This demand will not correspond to the demand for labor determined by the firm in the short run. For the firm will alter the employment of labor under a given stock of capital to adjust the level of production to the volume of sales occuring in the product market. The investment function, which explains the behavior of investment in the short run, will be closely related to the long run optimizing behavior of the firm, but the firm's demand for labor will not be related directly to it.

---

17) We have ever developed in other occasion a theory of investment determination through the equality of the demand for and supply of money, which showed that firms' investment would be determined in the process for establishing the equilibria of their plans of asset holdings. See S. Fujino: Business Cycles in Japan — A Theoretical, Statistical, and Historical Analysis of Cyclical Processes of Economic Development — (in Japanese), 1965, Ch. 9~10. The analysis of investment in this study was criticized in T. Negishi: The Supply of Money, Innovations, and the Business Cycle in Japan, Journal of Finance, Vol. 23, Dec. 1968, pp. 875-886. Negishi's criticism is that our theory of investment determination is same in its implication as that of Patinkin. We think that our analysis differs from Patinkin's one. The investment function presented here is a further development of it and it, we believe, shows clearly the difference between our and Patinkin's theory.

CHAPTER 2

BASIC RELATIONS OF A NEO-KEYNESIAN THEORY

2. 1 Towards A Neo-Keynesian Theory

After World War II, various fields of economic theory have been remarkably developed. Among them we could single out the theory of economic growth and monetary theory has having important achievements. Numerous studies on economic growth which have been published during the post-war period form one of the main fields in economic theory. This primary interest is due to the fact that many countries have experienced rapid growth and have attached great weight to growth in their economic planning. We might say that one of the significant accomplishments of growth theory was the transformation of the static theory of macro-economics to a long run dynamic theory, although the development of multi-sector analyses was no less important.

On the other hand, in the early post-war period the prevailing Keynesian Revolution fostered a post-Keynesian economics in which the emphasis was placed on real variables and the importance of monetary factors minimized. Thus monetary theory remained stagnant. In the latter half of the 1950's, however, a reaction began to occur. Namely, M. Friedman and the Chicago School presented the new theory of quantity of money,[1] and its introduction stimulated the appearance of many studies on the demand function for money. At the same time J. Tobin and other economists attempted to base the theory of demand for money on the maximizing behavior of economic units within the general theory of demand for assets.[2]

---

1) M. Friedman: The Quantity Theory of Money — A Restatement, Studies in the Quantity Theory of Money edited by M. Friedman, 1956, pp. 3-21.

2) J. Tobin: Liquidity Preference as Behavior Towards Risk, Review of Economic Studies, Feb. 1958, pp. 65-86.

Furthermore, the development of monetary theory was enlivened by studies of Don Patinkin, J. G. Gurley and E. S. Shaw, etc..[3]

When these two streams of studies had reached a certain stage of development, they began to penetrate each other. The result appeared as studies on the theory of monetary growth. Here we have on the one hand, studies on the neo-classical theory of monetary growth made by J. Tobin, D. Levhari and Don Patinkin, H. Johnson, M. Inage, M. Sidrauski, and so on, and on the other hand studies on the Keynesian theory of monetary growth presented by J. L. Stein, H. Rose and so forth.[4]

It seems, however, that there are still some unresolved problems in the theory of monetary growth.

At the first place, the literature does not succeed in explaining inflation closely connected with the short run mechanism of the economy, although attempts are made to explain the behavior of the rate of inflation. In addition it is difficult to identify in the various studies the relationship between monetary growth and business cycles, in spite of the fact that both are closely connected with

---

3) Don Patinkin: Money, Interest and Prices, first edition, 1956. J. G. Gurley and E. S. Shaw: Money in a Theory of Finance, 1960.

4) J. Tobin: Money and Economic Growth, Econometrica, Oct. 1965, pp. 671-684. J. Tobin: The Neutrality of Money in Growth Models: A Comment, Economica, Feb. 1957, pp. 69-72. H. Johnson: The Neo-classical One-Sector Growth Model — A Geometrical Exposition and Extension to a Monetary Economy, Economica, Aug. 1966, pp. 265-287. H. Johnson: The Neutrality of Money in Growth Models — A Reply, Economica, Feb. 1967, pp. 73-74. H. Johnson: Essays in Monetary Economy, 1967, pp. 143-178. D. Levhari and D. Patinkin: The Role of Money in a Simple Growth Model, American Economic Review, Sept. 1968, pp. 713-753. M. Sidrauski: Rational Choice and Patterns of Growth in a Monetary Economy, American Economic Review, May. 1967, pp. 534-544. M. Sidrauski: Inflation and Economic Growth, Journal of Political Economy, Dec. 1967, pp. 796-810. J. L. Stein: Money and Capacity Growth, Journal of Political Economy, Oct. 1966, pp. 451-465. J. L. Stein and K. Nagatani: Stabilization Policies in a Growing Economy, Review of Economic Studies, April. 1969, pp. 165-183. J. L. Stein: 'Neo-classical' and 'Keynes-Wicksell' Monetary Growth Models, Journal of Money, Credit and Banking, May. 1969, pp. 153-171. K. Nagatani: A Monetary Growth Model with Variable Employment, Journal of Money, Credit and Banking, May. 1969, pp. 188-206. H. Rose: Unemployment in a Theory of Growth, International Economic Review, Sept. 1966, pp. 260-282.

each other in the real world. An intrinsic theory of economic dynamics is expected to simultaneously explain business cycles, inflation which mainly arises through the short-run mechanism of the economy, and monetary growth, where we are concerned with secular inflation. Or at least it should make clear relationships among the various aspects of economic fluctuations in its attempt to unravel each of them.

Secondly, what kind of investment function should we employ ? It is well known that the neo-classical theory of monetary growth has no independent investment function. On the other hand, there appears to be an investment function, derived from Keynes' theory of investment, in the Keynesian theory of monetary growth. In Chapter 1, however, we pointed out that Keynes' theory of investment contains many weaknesses. And we presented an alternative theory of the investment function. In the following chapters, we shall attempt to explain various aspects of economic fluctuations in terms of this investment function.

Thirdly, how should we conceive of the substance of steady state growth so frequently used in studies on the theory of monetary growth ? This is, of course, a matter of definition. But may we adopt any arbitrary definition of it ? It seems necessary to take into consideration those definitions which will ultimately prove useful in theoretically explaining the observed process of monetary growth.

The growth steady state is frequently defined in the studies on the theory of monetary growth by the following two conditions; the rate of growth of the degree of capital intensity is zero, and the rate of growth of the ratio of real stock of money to capital stock (or the ratio of real stock of money to labor or the ratio of real stock of money to real output) is zero. When the rate of growth of capital intensity is zero, it does not matter whether we suppose the rate of growth of the money-capital ratio, or the money-labor ratio, or the money-output ratio to be zero.

Historically speaking, the degree of capital intensity has increased. Therefore, if we want to explain the actual behavior of the economic system in the long run by means of steady state growth, this should be reflected in the model. If we assume labor-augmenting technical progress, the degree of capital intensity with respect to natural labor will increase under the above definition of steady state growth, while intensity measured in terms of efficiency unit remains constant. Therefore, we might approach the real world by that definition.

But, when we suppose that the rate of growth of the money-capital ratio is zero, the rate of growth of real stock of money should be equal to the natural rate of growth in the steady state. Since the money-capital ratio has increased historically, it is difficult to get a suitable description of the historical course of economic growth by means of the above definition. Gurley and Shaw attempt on the basis of Enthoven's analysis to explain the rising tendency of the ratios of financial assets to income by supposing that the observed process corresponds to a coverging process to the steady state.[5] However, such a supposition must assume a very long coverging period to the steady state, since the ratios of financial assets to income have been rising for about one hundred years. On defining steady state growth we should keep this point well in mind.

And finally, it seems necessary to specify clearly what kind of money we deal with and also what kind money supply channels we include in our model of monetary growth. Recent studies on monetary growth distinguish between inside and outside money, based on the Gurley-Shaw study, with the supply of outside money usually given. The distinction between both types of money is definitely useful. But is it valid to exclude inside money from our analysis for the reason that it is canceled within the economy ? There is H. Johnson's criticism regarding the exclusion of inside money.[6] And it seems important that effects of inside money on

---

5) J. G. Gurley and E. Shaw: Money in a Theory of Finance, 1960, ch. 4. A. C. Enthoven: A Neo-classical Model of Money, Debt and Economic Growth, J. G. Gurley and E. Shaw: Ibid., pp. 303-359.

6) H. Johnson: Inside Money, Outside Money, Income, Wealth and Welfare in Monetary Theory, Journal of Money, Credit and Banking, Feb. 1969, pp. 30-45.

both sides of the national balance sheet be not counterbalanced because the influences on various sectors are not same in their absolute values.

On the other hand, it is frequently supposed in studies on monetary growth that money is supplied via transfer payments. But this channel of money supply seems to be scarsely used in the actual world. And it would be better to assume other routes, say, open market operations or deficit expenditures of the government in our analysis.

In what follows we shall construct a set of basic relationships, including the Keynesian theory of investment multiplier, on the basis of analyses developed thus far. And we shall attempt, with the benefit of these relationships, to explain: first, the process of cyclical growth in one of their working phases, secondly inflation, which would tend to appear in the neighborhood of full employment through the short-run mechanism of the economy, in the same cyclical phase but with some changes of our assumptions, and finally the process of monetary growth in the long-run tendency phase of the economy. In these analyses we shall utilize alternative assumptions regarding the wage-rate. When we investigate the process of cyclical growth, we shall assume that the money wage rate is rigid. But on analyzing inflation, we shall suppose that it recovers some flexibility. Furthermore, because prices change during the operation of a business cycle, the real wage rate would be altered even if the money wage-rate remained constant. And when we examine only business cycles peaks, we may assume that the economy reaches full employment which is achieved through the flexible real wage rate, which manifests itself between peak years. Thus we shall assume that the rate of real wage is flexible in the process of monetary growth to investigate the long-run tendency of the economy. Accordingly we shall develop our analyses along the set of three perspectives with our three alternative wage-rate conditions. This is one of the reasons why we attach to our theory the adjective, neo-Keynesian.

But we have a second reason. For we shall introduce, as pointed out earlier, an investment function which differs from that of Keynes' in order to construct our models.[7)]

We shall distinguish between short-run and long-run adjustments, and at the
same time the short-run and the long run steady states to explain cyclical growth
or inflation as well as to explain monetary growth as a long run tendency by a
set of basic relationships. Cyclical growth and inflation are explained by the
short run adjustment of the system. In the analysis of inflation we shall introduce a kind of short run steady state growth, where the supply of labor is not
always in equilibrium with the demand, and the steady state value of the rate of
inflation is not necessarily equal to the expected rate although the ratio of the
supply to the demand for labor and the degree of capital intensity remain constant, and the demand for and supply of products are in equilibrium. On the other
hand, in our analysis of monetary growth we shall describe movements of our system in terms of the long run adjustment, investigating characteristics of the
long run steady state growth. On investigating the short run and the long run
adjustments, we shall distinguish between the short run and the long run conditions affecting the formation of the expected rate of inflation. And we shall
assume that the system is not always at full employment in the short run, but it
is always at full employment in the long run, because the real wage rate recovers
flexibility there.

2. 2   Basic Relationships of A Neo-Keynesian Theory

The economy we are concerned with is assumed to consist of three sectors,
firm, household and government, although we shall sometimes introduce foreign
transactions into our analysis. The firm or business sector, we shall assume,
holds the entire capital stock and produces a single product by employing labor.

---

7) J. Williamson designates his model as neo-Keynesian in the sense that it pre-
supposes the multiplier process as well as the market mechanism by which the
equilibrium level of employment is automatically recovered. See J. Williamson:
A Simple Neo-Keynesian Growth Model, Review of Economic Studies, April. 1970,
pp. 157-171.

We assume that the product can either be used as consumption goods or as capital goods, and that it is permanently durable when it is used as capital goods. It is also assumed that the business firm sector holds money balance in addition to the above mentioned capital stock, and that their holdings are financed by means of the supply of securities. Therefore the firm's saving and net worth are zero respectively.

The household sector, we shall assume, obtains income by supplying labor to the business sector and by holding securities issued by the firm. In addition we shall assume later that it receives transfer payments from the government sector. We shall suppose that households purchase consumption goods by spending their incomes, a part of which forms positive saving. And the household sector, we shall assume, purchases securities and holds money as a form of saving.

Finally, the government sector is assumed to supply money to both the business and the household sectors through either the purchase of securities issued by firms or the purchase of products (i.e., deficit expenditures). We shall suppose that the earnings received by the government on its securities holdings is handed to households as transfer payments. Therefore, income generated by the business sector accrues entirely to households.

Our analysis of investment behavior in Chapter 1 was concerned with the representative firm. We shall suppose that it is applicable to the firm sector as a whole. And we use the same notations here, with the understanding that the variables are scaled upward by the number of firms. Thus the production function of the business sector is represented by

(2. 1) $Y_r = F(K, N)$,

where Y_r is linear homogeneous with respect to K and N. Let us suppose that technical progress is Harrod neutral. Therefore, labor input N is measured in terms of efficiency unit. Denote labor productivity (Y_r/N) by y and the degree of capital intensity (K/N) by k. Then we can rewrite equation (2. 1) as follows;

(2. 2) $y = y(k)$.

We shall assume that this production function is well-behaved.[8] When taking into account equations (1. 31) and (1. 32), the investment function is given by

$$(2.\ 3)\qquad \frac{I_r}{K} = \alpha[\ \frac{M}{pK.g[\ y'/(\theta - \pi_e)\ ]} - 1\ ],$$

where I_r expresses real investment, M the expected money balance of firms, p prices, g the ratio of firms' demand for real money to capital stock, y' the expected marginal productivity of capital at the current degree of capital intensity, π_e the expected rate of inflation, and θ the subjective discount rate of the typical firm. In the short run we shall assume, for simplicity:

$$(2.\ 4)\qquad \frac{M}{pK} = G(\ \frac{M_S}{pK}\ ),\qquad G' > 0,$$

where M_S is the supply of money. Therefore we can obtain from equations (2. 3) and (2. 4) the following:

$$(2.\ 5)\qquad \frac{I_r}{K} = \alpha[\ \frac{G(\ M_S/pK\ )}{g[\ y'/(\theta - \pi_e)\ ]} - 1\ ].$$

In the long run, however, we might suppose that M moves proportionally with pK, because growth of the economy would lead firms to anticipate an increase in M. Consequently (M/pK), which we denote by L^f, would be constant, taking the place of $G(M_S/pK)$ in equation (2. 5) in the long run.

Before proceeding with our analysis, let us place some restrictions on the subjective discount rate of the firm. We might suppose that the nominal rate θ is constant in the short run. But we would have to suppose that the real rate

---

8) That is, we assume that $y(0) = 0$, $y(k) > 0$, for $0 < k < \infty$, $y(\infty) = \infty$, $y'(0) = \infty$, $y'(k) > 0$ for $0 < k < \infty$, $y'(\infty) = 0$, and $y''(k) < 0$.

$(\theta - \pi_e)$ has some relationship to the market rate of real interest i_R, and that the former is changed so as to correspond to the change in the latter, in the long run. Denote $(\theta - \pi_e)$ by θ_R. And let us also assume that θ_R is an increasing function of i_R in the long run, which is expressed by the following relationship;

$$(2.6) \qquad \theta_R = \overline{\theta}_R(i_R) + \theta_R^*, \qquad \overline{\theta}_R' > 0,$$

where θ_R^* is the steady state value of θ_R, and is assumed to be equal to the steady state value of i_R, which we denote by i_R^*. Since it is natural to assume that θ_R is equal to θ_R^*, when i_R equals i_R^*, we shall suppose that $\overline{\theta}_R(i_R^*) = 0$. Thus, the firm's demand for real money (expressed as the ratio to capital stock) is given by g under a given θ in the short run. In the long run, however, it is a function of i_R through θ_R, where it is increased through the decrease in (y'/θ_R) when i_R is raised.

Next, let us specify the behavioral equations of the household sector. The demand for real money by the household is, we suppose, of the Keynesian type, so that it is a decreasing function of the real rate of interest and an increasing function of real income.

$$(2.7) \qquad m^h = m^h(i_R, y), \qquad m_1^h < 0, \qquad m_2^h > 0,$$

where m^h expresses the demand for money per efficiency unit of labor.

We should note an important point regarding the demand for money in general, i.e. the aggregate of firm and household demands. There is an upward shift of the demand function for money associated with the monetization of the economy. That is, when we are concerned with movements of the demand for money over a long lapse of time, we would have to take into consideration an additional factor affecting it. For the sake of explanative convenience, let us consider an imaginary economy consisting of a monetized and a non-monetized sector. In this case the monetized sector means a sector where purchasers clear transactions by means of money.[9] Now let us suppose that the degree of monetization, expressed by the weight of income produced in the monetized sector to the total income of this economy, is increased. This implies that the money-income ratio rises with the advance of monetization.

Thus, if the degree of monetization is uniform in any part of our economy under consideration at a given point of time, but rises through time, we would have to suppose that both the firms' and the households' demand functions for money shift upward uniformly. We express the shift parameter by

$$(2.8) \quad \Phi_M = \Phi_M(t), \quad \Phi_M' > 0.$$

Thus we need to multiply each of g and m^h by Φ_M to obtain the effective demand functions for money. To appropriately do so, however, we must introduce into our model of the economy firms and households existing in the non-monetized part, whose behaviors would be different from those of firms and households in the monetized part. This complicates our analysis. Therefore for simplicity we suppose an economy completely monetized, and retain the demand functions for money in the above assumed forms. And in order to make this completely monetized economy correspond more closely to the real world, we suppose that the observed supply of money deflated by Φ_M corresponds to the supply of money in a completely monetized economy.

On the other hand, over time the development of financial institutions diminishes the amount of money balance required to perform a given amount of transactions. This development could be thought as a kind of money augmenting technical progress. We express this factor by

$$(2.9) \quad \Phi_F = \Phi_F(t), \quad \Phi_F' > 0.$$

---

9) This definition is given in R. W. Goldsmith: Financial Structure and Development, 1969, p. 304.

Thus, money balance in terms of efficiency units will be equal to the actual balance of money times Φ_F.

Taking into account these two factors, we suppose that the supply of money in our economy, M_S, equals that in the real world, which we express by $\overline{M}_S$, multiplied by Φ_F and deflated by Φ_M, i.e., $M_S = \overline{M}_S(\Phi_F/\Phi_M)$. In the following analysis, we shall assume that the rate of growth of Φ_M is greater than that of Φ_F. The influences of Φ_M and Φ_F will especially important in Chapter 5, and we shall neglect them in our analyses of cyclical growth and inflation in Chapters 3 and 4.

Let us now examine saving behavior. In our economy the household sector saves a positive amount of its income. The ratio of real saving in the household S_r to capital stock K is expressed as follows;

$$(2.\ 10)\quad \frac{S_r}{K} = s\ \frac{y}{k},$$

where s is the ratio of S_r to Y_r. We may suppose that the saving ratio s is constant in the short run as well as in the long run. Thus we have

$$(2.\ 11)\quad s = \text{constant}.$$

Finally, we should investigate how the expected rate of inflation is formed. Because it appears in the demand for money function and the investment function of the business sector, what we have to examine is the rate of inflation expected by firms in their assets holdings planning. Let us introduce here what we call the Keynesian expectation hypothesis. Keynes assumed that when the rate of interest is lower (higher) than a safe level, people expect that the rate of interest will rise (fall) in the future, because the current rate is too low (high). Keynes' conception of liquidity preference includes this expectation hypothesis as one of its key components. His reasoning can be divided into the following three stages. (1) The demand for money is an increasing function of the expected rate of interest (therefore a decreasing function of the expected price of securities). On the other hand, (2) the rate of interest would be expected to fall, when the market rate is higher than the safe rate, <u>vice versa</u>. Therefore, (3) the demand for money is a decreasing function of the rate of interest.[10] What we are concerned with here is the second stage. Denote the market rate of interest by i, the expected rate by i_e, and the safe rate by i_n. Then we can express the proposition as follows;

$$(2.\ 12) \qquad i_e - i = \bar{\beta}^*(1 - i_n), \qquad \bar{\beta}^* < 0.$$

Or we rewrite equation (2. 12) to get

$$(2.\ 13) \qquad i_e = (1 + \bar{\beta}^*)i - \bar{\beta}^* i_n.$$

In order to obtain the third proposition from the first and equation (2. 13), $\bar{\beta}^*$ should be less than (-1).

If we apply the Keynesian expectation hypothesis to the formation of the expected rate of inflation, the following relationship will be supposed among the expected rate of inflation π_e, the actual rate π and the normal rate π_n;[11]

$$(2.\ 14) \qquad \pi_e - \pi = \bar{\beta}(\pi - \pi_n), \qquad \bar{\beta} < -1.$$

or we can obtain from equation (2. 14)

$$(2.\ 15) \qquad \pi_e = \beta\pi + (1 - \beta)\pi_n,$$

---

10) Keynes denotes the rate of interest by r, and asserts as follows; "what matters is not the <u>absolute</u> level of r but the degree of its divergence from what is considered a fairly <u>safe</u> level of r, having regard to those calculations of probability which are being relied on. ... if the general view as to what is a safe level of r is unchanged, every fall in r reduces the market rate relatively to the 'safe' rate and therefore increases the risk of illiquidity." J. M. Keynes: <u>The General Theory of Employment, Interest and Money</u>, 1936, pp. 201-202.

11) We may employ the 'normal' rate instead of the 'safe' rate used by Keynes.

where $\beta = (1 + \bar{\beta})$, so that $\beta < 0$. For simplicity, we assume β is constant.

In the short run analysis we distinguish between π_e and π_n. Neverthless, we might suppose that π_e coincides with π_n in the long run, which implies that π is equal to π_e or π_n.

Briefly, let us summarize our basic relationships. First there is the production function (2. 2). For convenience we shall redesignate it as

$$(2. 16) \quad y = y(k).$$

Next, when money is supplied through open market operations, which means that government purchases securities issued by firms or held by households, we obtain the following basic relationships as short run equilibrium conditions for money and for output, respectively.

$$(2. 17) \quad g\left(\frac{y'}{\theta - \pi_e} \right) + \frac{1}{k} m^h (i_R, y) = L_S,$$

$$(2. 18) \quad \frac{I_r}{K} = \alpha\left[\frac{G(L_S)}{g[y'/(\theta - \pi_e)]} - 1 \right] = s\, \frac{y}{k} = \frac{S_r}{K},$$

where L_S is equal to (M_S/pK), i.e., $(\Phi_F \bar{M}_S/\Phi_M pK)$ and θ and s are constant, respectively. And we must emphasize that y' is the expected marginal productivity of capital.

On the other hand, in the long run we have

$$(2. 19) \quad g[\, y'/\theta_R(i_R)\,] + \frac{1}{k} m^h(i_R, y) = L_S,$$

$$(2. 20) \quad \alpha\left[\frac{L_f}{g[\, y'/\theta_R(i_R)\,]} - 1 \right] = s\, \frac{y}{k}.$$

If the supply of money is altered through deficit expenditures on the part of the government (or via a surplus in the international balance of payments), we have to revise somewhat equation (2. 18) or equation (2. 20).

Furthermore, the expected rate of inflation is formed in the short run by

(2. 21) $\quad \pi_e = \beta\pi + (1 - \beta)\pi_n.$

In the long run, however, we suppose

(2. 22) $\quad \pi_e = \pi_n = \pi.$

Regarding the demand for and supply of labor, we suppose that, generally speaking, the economy is at a stage of under-employment in the short run because of the rigidity of the money wage rate. In our analysis of inflation, however, we shall alter the presupposition by assuming that the money wage rate becomes flexible when the economy approaches close to full employment. And we shall suppose in the long run that the real wage rate is so flexible that full employment is always attained.

Our basic relationships are equations (2. 16), (2. 17), (2. 18), and (2. 21) in the short run, and equations (2. 16), (2. 19), (2. 20) and (2. 22) in the long run. And we can obtain our models of cyclical growth, inflation and monetary growth by adding some subsidiary relationships to our basic ones (or by revising the basic relationships in some cases).

CHAPTER 3

A NEO-KEYNESIAN THEORY OF GROWTH CYCLE

3. 1   A Model of Growth Cycle

In analyzing business cycles, economists have usually come to graspe the
phenomenon in terms of cyclical fluctuations in the absolute values of economic variables, such as output and prices. And economic statisticans decompose
economic time-series into its cyclical and time-trend parts, investigating each
seperately. However, business cycles appear to be closely connected with economic growth, and both of these phenomena should be analyzed simultaneously in theoretical studies as well as in statistical examinations.

In an economy which has experienced rapid growth, such as the Japanese economy, various economic variables scarcely manifest cyclical fluctuations in their
absolute levels. This does not mean that there is no cycle in the economy. Because of the rapid growth, sluggish behavior is reflected only in the fall of the
rate of growth of an economic variable, and not its absolute level.

Therefore, it may be more relevant to understand cycles in terms of cyclical
fluctuations of the rate of growth of, say, output than of its absolute level.
Thus a growth cycle model which relates business cycles to economic growth is in
order. We shall investigate cyclical fluctuations from this point of view.

Let us now construct a model of growth cycle by taking into account our short
run basic relationships. For this purpose we should elaborate on how the normal
rate of inflation is formed and on how the actual rate is changed.

First let us investigate the behavior of the normal expected rate of inflation. It seems that the rate of inflation, judged as normal, will move in the
same direction as the change in the actual rate. And the magnitude of the response coefficient will depend on the length of unit period we choose, i.e., the
longer the unit period, the nearer it will be to unity. In the short run it is
less than unity.

This relationship between the expected rate and the actual rate of inflation prevails only when the actual rate is changing within a certain range. When π rises above or falls below this range, however, the relationship is altered. If π increases substantially, for example, the level of π would be judged as abnormally high, so that the normal rate would not be correspondingly raised. Similarly, when π is unusually low, the normal rate would not be diminished below a certain limit.

Such a relationship between π_n and π as shown in Fig. 3-1. Namely, when π is located between π^* and π^{**}, $d\pi_n/d\pi$ is greater than zero and less than unity, but when π is raised beyond a positive value π^*, $d\pi_n/d\pi$ turns to zero, and the normal rate stays at π_n^*. Similarly, when π falls below a negative value π^{**}, $d\pi_n/d\pi$ changes to zero, and π_n remains at the value of π_n^{**}.

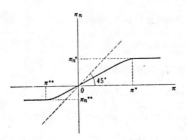

Fig. 3-1

It is probably true that the absolute value of π^{**} is less than π^*.

Based on the preceeding examination, we can derive relationships between $(1 - \beta)\pi_n$ and π and between $(- \beta\pi)$ and π as shown in Fig. 3-2. It is evident

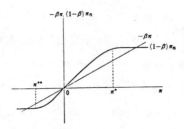

Fig. 3-2

1869690

from equation (2. 15) that π_e is nothing but the difference between $(1 - \beta)\pi_n$ and $(- \beta\pi)$, so that we are able to obtain a relationship between π_e and π as shown in Fig. 3-3. In this case $(1 - \beta)$ is greater than $(- \beta)$ because of our supposition. And in addition, we shall assume that the absolute value of $(1 - \beta)$ π_n is greater than that of $(- \beta\pi)$ in the neighborhood of the origin.

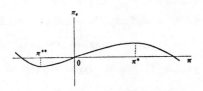

Fig. 3-3

According to Fig. 3-3, π_e is dampened when π is in excess of π^*. As mentioned in Chapter 2, the expected rate of inflation we are concerned with is the one formed in the business sector. And the expected rate is with regards to prices at which firms can sell products in the future when their investments have matured and are producing additional output. Accordingly, an abnormally high level in the current rate of inflation causes, we can say, firms to feel anxious about the future rate, so that π_e responds rather negatively to the change in π.[1]

---

1) The adaptive expectation hypothesis is frequently adopted with respect to the expected rate of inflation. The reason why we do not use it and adopt instead the Keynesian expectation hypothesis is as follows: When we were empirically examining the Japanese demand function for money, which includes the expected rate of inflation as an explanatory variable, we found that real money balances were larger than those which are inferred from the levels of the expected rate of inflation based on the adaptive expectation hypothesis at the end of booms. In his analysis of the demand for money in a period of hyperinflation, P. Cagan faced similar difficulties in some of observations near the end of hyperinflations. These facts support the contention that the adaptive expectation hypothesis is no longer valid for explaining the behavior of the expected rate of inflation toward the end of booms or hyperinflations. If we adopt the hypothesis presented in the text, however, we could resolve the above mentioned discrepancies. It is for this reason that we employ the Keynesian hypothesis rather than the adaptive expectation hypothesis. See P. Cagan: The Monetary Dynamics of Hyperinflation, Studies in the Quantity Theory of Money, edited by M. Friedman, 1956, pp. 25-117, esp. pp. 55-57.

Now, let us examine short run price and quantity adjustments in order to derive a relationship which characterizes the behavior of the actual rate of inflation. According to Keynes' theory of the investment multiplier, when investment
is increased, i.e., when excess demand appears in the product market, the adjustment between the demand for and supply of output is brought about through the
change in income. In general, there will be changes in real output as well as
prices. In his Treatise on Money published prior to the General Theory, Keynes
assumes that excess demand is absorbed into windfall profits through the temporary rise in prices to such an extent that no change in output occurs. But this
assumption neglects the possibility that excess demand is adjusted through change
in product inventories or orders backlogs. If firms react to excess demand by
working down product inventories, prices will not rise. This is the case of an-
ticipative production. On the other hand, if firms absorb the demand in excess
of the optimal amount of orders by increasing their order backlogs at the current
prices, in the case of production-to-order, prices would not rise immediately in
this case, too. Consequently, price adjustment would not respond rapidly to excess demand. And the demand for and supply of output would be balanced mainly by
the change in output via either inventory or order backlog adjustments. Thus we
might express quantity adjustment as

$$(3.\ 1)\qquad \frac{d(Y_r/K)}{dt} \Big/ \left(\frac{Y_r}{K} \right) = a\left(\frac{I_r - S_r}{K} \right), \qquad a > 0,$$

where a is a constant. (We neglect here government and external demand. Even if
we were to introduce them into our model, there will be no essential change in
the conclusions.)

On the other hand, what form does price adjustment take in the multiplier
process ? If excess demand is temporarily absorbed by changes in inventories or
in backlogs of orders, we may suppose that prices will fall (rise) when product
inventories increase beyond (fall below) a normal magnitude, or when backlogs of
orders fall below (increase beyond) a normal magnitude. Thus, if we take into

consideration both changes in inventories and in backlogs of orders together, then we obtain

(3. 2) $\dot{p} = \bar{\gamma} [\int_{-\infty}^{t}(I_r - S_r) \, d\tau + \bar{b}],$ $\bar{\gamma} = \text{const.} > 0,$

where $\bar{b}$ is the difference between the normal values of real inventories and real backlogs of orders. $\int_{-\infty}^{t}(I_r - S_r)d\tau$ in equation (3. 2) is the difference between the cumulative real backlogs of orders and the cumulative real product inventories. In our analysis, however, we shall assume by the analogy of equation (3. 2) the following price adjustment:

(3. 3) $\pi = \gamma[\int_{-\infty}^{t}(\dfrac{I_r - S_r}{K}) \, d\tau + b],$ $\gamma = \text{const.} > 0,$

where b is constant. Then, we substitute equation (3. 1) into equation (3. 3) to obtain

(3. 4) $\pi = (\gamma/a) \log(Y_r/K) + \gamma[b - (1/a) \log(Y_r/K)_0],$

where $(Y_r/K)_0$ is the initial output-capital ratio. Generalizing equation (3. 4), we have

(3. 5) $\pi = \pi(Y_r/K),$ $\pi' > 0.$

Now, taking into account our investment function of equation (2. 18), our relationship between π_e and π, and equation (3. 5), and differentiating (I_r/K) by (Y_r/K) under a given expected marginal productivity of capital and a given real money-capital ratio, we get

(3. 6) $\dfrac{\partial(I_r/K)}{\partial(Y_r/K)} = - \dfrac{\alpha}{g^2} [g' \dfrac{d\pi_e}{d\pi} \cdot \dfrac{d\pi}{d(Y_r/K)} \cdot \dfrac{y'}{(\theta - \pi_e)^2} G].$

$(- \alpha g'/g^2 . d\pi/d(Y_r/K) . y'/(\theta - \pi_e)^2 . G)$ in the right-hand side of equation (3. 6) is positive, so that the sign of $\partial(I_r/K)/\partial(Y_r/K)$ is the same as that of $(d\pi_e/d\pi)$. Therefore the relationship between (I_r/K) and (Y_r/K) can be illustrated, for example, by curves $(I_r/K)_0$, $(I_rK)_1$ and $(I_r/K)_2$ in Fig. 3-4. And since the saving ratio s is constant, the relationship between (S_r/K) and (Y_r/K) will be a straight line like the (S_r/K) line in Fig. 3-4.

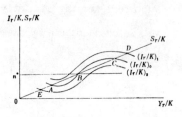

Fig. 3-4

In Fig. 3-4 net investment I_r is assumed to be positive. It was made clear in Chapter 1 that the main reason for this is Harrod neutral technical progress, which is what we assume.

Formally speaking, the above saving-investment relation coincides completely with Kaldor's model of the trade cycle.[2] But, of course, our reasons for a non-linear investment function are quite different from Kaldor's. And it should especially be noted that investment has to be negative in some situations in order that the trade cycle is generated in the Kaldor model. Similarly, in Goodwin's models, investment must turn negative for a considerably long period to generate cycles.[3] And it is clear from observed cycles that the presupposition of negative net investment is very unrealistic. In the following analysis, cyclical

2) N. Kaldor: A Model of the Trade Cycle, Economic Journal, Vol. 50, March. 1940, pp. 78-92.

3) R. M. Goodwin: The Nonlinear Accelerator and the Persistence of Business Cycles, Econometrica, Vol. 19, Jan. 1951, pp. 1-17. R. M. Goodwin: A Model of Cyclical Growth, The Business Cycles in the Post-War World, edited by E. Lundberg, 1955, pp. 203-221.

growth is generated without negative net investment. In our model, growth of the
system is warranted by the existence of permanently positive rate of capital accumulation which fluctuates cyclically.

3. 2   Technical Progress, Innovation and Growth Cycles

Now let us turn to Fig. 3-4 to investigate the behavior of our model. Suppose that the investment curve is initially $(I_r/K)_0$. Then A and C are stable e-
quilibrium points, but B an unstable equilibrium point. Let us suppose that the
economy is at A. We have to take into consideration two factors here. First,
whether is a change in the expected marginal productivity of capital and secondly,
if there is a change in the real money-capital ratio L_S, both of which were supposed to be given in the differentiation in equation (3. 6).

Let us examine the first factor. This is closely connected with innovation.
Technological innovation is a process of utilizing and digesting technological
possibilities accumulated so far in a concentrated manner. Accordingly the realization of technical progress comes in intervals, even if technical progress itself appears uniformly from year to year. Let us examine this process in terms
of Harrod neutral technical progress presupposed in our model.

Denote labor productivity and the degree of capital intensity with respect
to labor in terms of natural units by $\bar{y}$ and $\bar{k}$, respectively, in order to distinguish them from the efficiency unit measures. The marginal productivity of capital is same on each productivity curves at a given value of (Y_r/K). Therefore,
in Fig. 3-5 we have productivity curves where the slopes of the productivity
curves at B, D and G or those at A, E and H are same.

Suppose that a firm does not recognize accumulated technical progress until
it reaches a certain magnitude. Furthermore, suppose once the firm is aware of
technical advances, it devotes itself to the complete exhaustion of the technological possibilities. This is an assumption for expository simplicity. In practice firms will immediately incorporate technical progress, which we assume is
continuously occuring. But we ignore this point here.

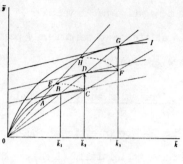

Fig. 3-5

In Fig. 3-5, let us suppose that the typical firm is at point C and knows of
the existence of a productivity curve passing through E, D and F which represents
the upper limit of all new productivity curves located above the current productivity curve ABC. Then the expected marginal productivity of capital is shown
by the slope of the tangent to curve EDF at D. Thus there would be an increase in
the expected marginal productivity of capital. We shall assume that the firm can
approach the new productivity curve EDF only by means of additional investment.
This implies that only with the aid of new investments can the firm inject new
technologies into its existing capital stock. Through this assumption we avoid
the difficult problems associated with disembodied and embodied technical pro-
gresses.

When the expected marginal productivity of capital is enhanced in this fash-
ion, the (I_r/K) curve in Fig. 3-4 will shift upwards, say, from the $(I_r/K)_0$ curve
to the $(I_r/K)_1$ curve. Then, Y_r/K will rise so that the economy will move toward
D in Fig. 3-4. This process will be characterized as a movement, say, from C to
E in Fig. 3-5. The expected marginal productivity of capital is represented, in
this case, by the tangent on each point along the segment of curve EDF starting
from D and arriving at E, so that it will be raised further in the process of
moving from C to E.

Suppose the system reaches an upper stable equilibrium point like D in Fig.

3-4, when it arrives at E in Fig. 3-5. As long as it remains at D, the expected marginal productivity of capital will remain constant. As long as there are no more technological spurts the expected marginal productivity of capital will be identical to the actual. One more factor has to be taken into account here, and this is the rate of growth of labor in terms of natural units, which we denote by n^*. We shall assume that it takes an intermediate value between the rates of capital accumulation corresponding to A and C in Fig. 3-4. In Fig. 3-4 its height is drawn such that it happens to coincide with the intermediate equilibrium point B in the $(I_r/K)_0$ curve. Or suppose that we choose the $(I_r/K)_0$ curve such that the height of B will coincide with n^*.

Now as the system moves from A to the upper equilibrium point D, the value of Y_r/K will increase, so that the degree of capital intensity $\bar{k}$ will fall. This means that the rate of growth of capital is less than that of employment. However the former is greater than the rate of growth of existing labor at D. Therefore after a certain time lapse full employment will have to be reached in the sense that all the existing labor will be employed. When capital is accumulated further after the economy has attained full employment, the degree of capital intensity $\bar{k}$ must necessarily increase. And therefore the expected as well as actual marginal productivities of capital will diminish. Thus the (I_r/K) curve will shift downwards in Fig. 3-4. And eventually the (I_r/K) curve will fall to the position of the $(I_r/K)_2$ curve, and the system will move towards E in Fig. 3-4. Meanwhile unemployment will appear. When the system reaches E in Fig. 3-4, the fall in Y_r/K will terminate because E is a stable equilibrium point. Also the degree of capital intensity $\bar{k}$ will cease to rise, and the system will stay at, say, F in Fig. 3-5. The expected and actual marginal productivities of capital will stop to fall.

While the above processes are going on, technical progress will be generated throughout the upward and downward movements of the business cycle. And a new technological frontier will be given, for instance, by the productivity curve HGI in Fig. 3-5 at the time when the system reaches point F. We might suppose that firms are not aware of new technological possibilities as long as the expected marginal productivity of capital is falling (or more generally speaking, rising and falling), and they start to search only after marginal productivity of capital movements have stopped. This is plausible since firms would be busy digesting and incorporating technological possibilities already known during the upward movement of the business cycle on the one hand, and would be occupied with adapting itself to the depressed conditions during the downward movement of the business cycle, on the other hand, so that they would not have enough time to seek new technological possibilities.

When the expected marginal productivity of capital ceases to move, however, firms would become concerned about the environment and would actively seek new technological possibilities. Under this assumption, the expected marginal productivity of capital will jump upward again, because firms will become cognizant of the existence of the new productivity curve HGI when the system has reached point F in Fig. 3-5. Thus the whole process repeats itself.

In Fig. 3-5, it is assumed that the values of (Y_r/K), and hence the magnitudes of the expected marginal productivity of capital, are the same at the end of each technological catching-up phase. And in addition, we assumed that values are also identical for each through of the growth cycle. Actually there are some differences among the values of Y_r/K at the turning points. But it appears that our approximation does not deviate significantly from reality.

The dynamic relation between the expected marginal productivity of capital y' and the output-capital ratio Y_r/K can be explained in terms of Fig. 3-6. Let us begin our discussion at point A, which corresponds to the through of the business cycle which we are considering. The expected marginal productivity of

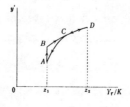

Fig. 3-6

capital is temporarily stationary at the z_1 value of Y_r/K. But subsequently it jumps upwards at z_1, and we observe a movement from A to B. The economy will eventually start an upward movement along the curve BCD. As Y_r/K increases, the expected marginal productivity of capital increases, thereby inducing a movement from B to D through C. And the economy will ultimately arrive at the turning point D, and thereafter the decrease in the expected marginal productivity of capital will induce a fall in Y_r/K as represented by the movement from D to A through C.

When the expected marginal productivity of capital shows cyclical fluctuations in accordance with changes in Y_r/K as shown above, the fluctuations will cause the (I_r/K) curve to shift, so that a growth cycle — the cyclical fluctuation in the rate of capital accumulation or the rate of growth of output — will be generated. We may say that this is nothing but the Schumpeterian explanation of cyclical growth.

3. 3   Change in Money Supply and the Growth Cycle

As shown above, we can explain the growth cycle process by the change in the expected marginal productivity of capital. But it seems that there is another factor which causes shift in the (I_r/K) curve, and therefore provides an alternative explanation of the growth cycle. This other determinant is the real money-capital ratio L_S, or more specifically, changes in this ratio. Although L_S includes the shift parameters Φ_M and Φ_F, we shall disregard them in our analysis of the growth cycle.

Among the various channels by which the money supply is altered, we are primarily interested in money supply changes induced by economic activities, in order to endogenously explain growth cycles. The change in money supply resulting from fluctuations in the balance of trade seems to be a prime channel for us to examine. Let us assume that there is no international movement of capital except for clearing the balance of trade account.

Suppose, for simplicity, that real import I_m is a constant proportion of real output Y_r, and that real export E_x so happens to bear a fixed relation to the capital stock K. And import is, we assume, less in the relatively low level of Y_r/K and greater in the relatively high level of Y_r/K than export.[4] This situation is illustrated in Fig. 3-7. We can safely assume that Y_r/K is low during a

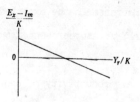

Fig. 3-7

depression and high during a boom. Since the balance of trade represents the entire international balance of payments, our balance of payments will be positive during a depression period, with the size of the surplus (the ratio of surplus to capital stock) gradually diminishing with the upward movement of the business cycle, and eventually turning negative.

The ratio of the money supply to capital stock L_S will be expressed in this case as follows;

$$(3.\ 7)\quad L_S = \frac{M_{S_0}}{p(t)K(t)} + \frac{1}{p(t)K(t)} \int_0^t p(\tau)[E_x(\tau) - I_m(\tau)]\ d\tau,$$

where M_{S_0} denotes the supply of money at the initial point. It is, of course, not equal to

$$\frac{M_{S_0}}{p_0 K_0} + \int_0^t [\frac{E_x(\tau) - I_m(\tau)}{K(\tau)}]\ d\tau,$$

---

4) If the contrary happens, the exchange rate is, we suppose, so altered that the situation we are refering to will be brought about.

where p_0 and K_0 are the initial values of p and K, respectively. But it seems
that this magnitude moves almost correspondingly to L_S, and that such a relationship between $[(E_x - I_m)/K]$ and L_S as shown in Fig. 3-8 can be observed, when Y_r/K
fluctuates cyclically over time.

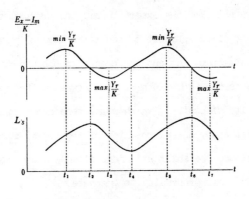

Fig. 3-8

When we introduce foreign trade into our system, the short run basic relationship (2. 18) should be revised. Under our assumptions the real export-
capital ratio E_x/K is constant and real import bears a fixed relationship to
real output Y_r, so that we can express the new relation between the demand for
and supply of output by shifting the (I_r/K) curve upwards by the constant (E_x/K)
and by raising the slope of the (S_r/K) line from s to $(s + I_m/K)$. Thus there is
no essential change in the shape of the saving-investment schedules in Fig. 3-4.
For convenience let us suppose that schedules revised in this manner are represented by the (I_r/K) curve and by the (S_r/K) line in Fig. 3-4.

Now let us start from point A in Fig. 3-4. L_S will increase at A, so that
the (I_r/K) curve will shift upwards through increases in the G function, inducing
an upward movement of the system. Suppose the (I_r/K) curve shifts, say, to the
location of $(I_r/K)_1$, so that the system will eventually move to the upper stable
equilibrium point. During the process, however, L_S will begin to decrease, so
that the (I_r/K) curve will begin to shift downwards. This will continue even

though Y_r/K begins to decrease. Therefore a movement to the lower stable equilibrium point will occur sooner or later.

We have examined separately the two factors which shift the (I_r/K) curve and generate the growth cycle process. Although these two factors appear to be independent on the surface, they in fact have a close relationship to each other. In section 3. 2 we assumed that the expected marginal productivity of capital would jump upward owing to firms' pursuit of new technological possibilities when technical knowledge has accumulated and the change in the expected marginal productivity of capital has terminated. In practice, however, the rise in the expected marginal productivity of capital, which would generate technological innovations, is frequently initiated by an upward shift of the (I_r/K) curve generated by an increase in L_S, because the shift will make firms' psychology optimistic, and therefore intensify their propensity to innovate.

On the other hand, technological innovations appearing in one cycle would prepare export increases for the next cycle. It was for the sake of showing this effect that we assumed a fixed ratio between export and capital stock. And if the export-capital ratio was significantly enhanced by innovations, L_S will cease to have an influence on movements of the (I_r/K) curve. The accumulation of international balance of payments surplus would, in this case, hasten to raise the parity of the currency of the economy we are concerned with. In our analysis, as mentioned in footnote 4, the accumulation of surplus or deficit is maintained by changes in the exchange-rate.

3. 4   Growth Cycles and Movements of The Rate of Interest

So far we have advanced our investigation by concentrating our attention principally on the short run basic relationship (2. 18). Let us now examine equation (2. 17) to describe movements of the rate of interest in the process of cyclical growth. For simplicity, we assume that the demand for money per labor in the household m^h is linear homogeneous of y. Then (m^h/k) is an increasing function of $y/k(= Y_r/K)$. When Y_r/K is changed under a given L_S, the real rate of interest i_R should be altered to equilibrate the demand for money with the supply as follows:

$$(3. 8) \quad \frac{\partial i_R}{\partial (Y_r/K)} = \frac{g' \dfrac{d\pi_e}{d\pi} \dfrac{d\pi}{d(Y_r/K)} \dfrac{y'}{(\theta - \pi_e)^2} + g' \dfrac{1}{(\theta-\pi_e)} \dfrac{\partial y'}{\partial (Y_r/K)} + \dfrac{\partial (m^h/k)}{\partial (Y_r/K)}}{-\dfrac{\partial (m^h/k)}{\partial i_R}}.$$

The denominator of the right-hand side of equation (3. 8) is positive. The second term of the numerator is negative, because $g' < 0$ and $\partial y'/\partial(Y_r/K) > 0$, and the third term is positive. Since $d\pi_e/d\pi$ could be positive or zero or negative, the first term of the numerator could be negative or zero or positive. Therefore we cannot determine the sign of the numerator. However, the numerator is nothing but the derivative of the total demand for money per capital with respect to Y_r/K. And we might suppose that it is positive. Then $\partial i_R/\partial (Y_r/K)$ should be positive.

Since the nominal rate of interest i is defined by the sum of the real rate of interest i_R and the expected rate of inflation π_e, we obtain

$$(3. 9) \quad \frac{\partial i}{\partial (Y_r/K)} = \frac{\partial i_R}{\partial (Y_r/K)} + \frac{d\pi_e}{d\pi} \frac{d\pi}{d(Y_r/K)}.$$

Here again the sign of $\partial i/\partial (Y_r/K)$ depends on that of $d\pi_e/d\pi$. And taking into consideration the relationship between π_e and π shown in Fig. 3-3, we might suppose as one possibility the $\overline{L}_1$ curve in Fig. 3-9 which depict the relationships between i and Y_r/K.[5] The lower $\overline{L}_i$ (i=1,2,3...) curve corresponds to a greater L_S, because

---

5) Even if the L_i curve is a decreasing or increasing function of Y_r/K in our concerned range of Y_r/K, the following examination is not altered fundamentally.

the rate of interest will fall as L_S increases.

Now if the movement of L_S corresponds to that of Y_r/K as shown in Fig. 3-8 and, in addition, if the maximum value (or minimum value) of L_S is always the same, being attained at a same magnitude of Y_r/K, then their relationship will be expressed by a circle as shown in the lower part of Fig. 3-9. Namely L_S will take an intermediate value L_2 between the maximum and the minimum, when Y_r/K takes the lowest value z_1, and will rise in accordance with the rise in Y_r/K, attaining the maximum L_3 at z_2. When Y_r/K increases further, L_S will begin to decrease, taking the intermediate value L_2 again at z_3. When Y_r/K diminishes below z_3, L_S will decrease at first, and will take the minimum L_1 at z_2, increasing thereafter to return to the starting point L_2 at z_1.

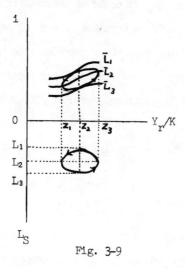

Fig. 3-9

When L_S moves, as shown above, in accordance with the change in Y_r/K, the rate of interest will change in conjunction with Y_r/K in the manner depicted by the arrows on the loop shown in the upper part of Fig. 3-9. Suppose the movement of Y_r/K starts from z_1. Then L_S is L_2 and i is on the $\overline{L}_2$ curve. When Y_r/K increases, the $\overline{L}_i$ curve will shift downwards due to the increase in L_S. And L_S becomes L_2 and i is on the $\overline{L}_3$ curve, when Y_r/K is at z_2. When Y_r/K increases further, L_S will start to fall, so that the $\overline{L}_i$ curve will shift upwards. At Y_r/K = z_3, i is again on the $\overline{L}_2$ curve. Since L_S continues to decrease with decreases

in Y_r/K after z_3, the $\overline{L}_i$ curve will shift upwards further so that i will continue
to rise. But before Y_r/K reaches z_2, i will reverse itself and continue to fall
even after Y_r/K arrives at the lowest level. Thus the nominal rate of interest
will follow the movement of Y_r/K, and therefore the business cycle in general,
with a time-lag.

The above investigated process of growth cycle conforms well with previous
studies, which are of both empirical and theoretical substance.[6]

---

6) S. Fujino: Business Cycles in Japan(in Japanese), 1965, esp. Ch. 23-26. S.
Fujino: Construction Cycles and Their Monetary-Financial Characteristics,
Economic Growth — The Japanese Experience Since The Meiji Era — edited by L.
R. Klein & K. Ohkawa, 1968, pp. 35-68.

CHAPTER 4

A NEO-KEYNESIAN THEORY OF INFLATION

4. 1   On a Dynamic Analysis of Inflation

The greatest changes in post-war national economic policies occurred in measures to achieve full employment, economic growth and a welfare state. The policies have been successful to a considerable extent in attaining these goals.
Although the business cycle which periodically disturbs capitalistic economies
has not yet disappeared from the economic scene, it is losing some of its dread-
ful repercussions because of the total demand adjustment measures aimed at full
employment. The unemployment experienced in the early 1930s has disappeared and
people's income have risen owing to growth inducing measures. Welfare measures
stabilize the lives of those who are less favored with direct benefits from the
growth economy. Behind the success of these policies, certain important changes
are being made in the mechanisms of the modern capitalistic economy.

In the first place, as a result of measures taken to ensure full employment,
aggregate demand is stabilized. This enables firms to sell their products more
easily. Firms in the capitalistic economy are exposed to risk associated with the
marketability of their products. But the risk burden is lessened with policy
measures to stabilize demand. This is all the more true when demand is stimulated
by growth measures. Even if demand is dampened by rising prices, total demand
adjustment measures are sufficient to dominate this type of demand decreases and
even provide conditions under which it is easy to raise prices.

Income increases enable people to maintain their demand even if prices rise.
In other words, it seems that with a significant rise in income, product demand
loses its price elasticity. Under this condition, it is easy and profitable for
firms to raise prices. Thus, as a result of full employment measures, a condition
is being created where firms can obtain what they want, that is, to set prices.
The supply price can be called the price required by firms, or in short the

required price. Full employment measures make it easy for firms to realize their requests.

Secondly, full employment, economic growth and welfare economy measures improved people's income and living standards, eliminating the necessity of working hard to make a living and providing at the same time a wider selection of job and leisure. Under these circumstances, people have come to make subjective revaluations of their own labor value and to demand the higher wage rates that they feel they deserve. And it has become easier for them to achieve their demands.

If the economy attains near full employment, an increase in wage rates will be triggered, even if supply exceeds demand in the labor market. While wage rates show rigidity in some parts of the labor market where excess supply exists, wage rates rise in parts where excess demand exists. The greater the bargaining power of labor unions, the stronger this tendency becomes. From this, inflation seems to occur in the following pattern:

(1) When full employment is nearly reached, wage rates begin to rise with some flexibility.

(2) This rise in wages is reflected by increases in the firms' required price.

(3) Since the required price can be easily obtained in product markets, even if the supply and demand relation is well balanced, market prices rise.

(4) In the case where the required wage rate is dependent on the price level, the realization of required wage rates accentuates price rises.

Inflation which occurs this way can be called "employment inflation" and is closely related to the changes in the market structure which have taken place in connection with full employment measures. That is, employment inflation is a sustained rise in the price level caused by the transition of money wage rate from rigidity to flexibility.

It is well known that one of the distinctive features of the Keynesian theory is the presumption that the money wage rate is rigid. We adhered to this in our neo-Keynesian theory of growth cycle, where we assumed that under employment is the general tendency in an economy characterized by rigidity of the money wage rate. When the money wage rate becomes flexible under near full employment conditions, there will exist a possibility that the growth cycle process transforms into a process of secular inflation. It is further possible that we have inflation even under stagnation accompanied by unemployment, i.e. "stagflation". The purpose of this chapter is to clarify the mechanisms of employment inflation and of stagflation.

4. 2   Model of Employment Inflation

1. Price Adjustment Equation

In order to build a model of employment inflation, let us first reexamine the price adjustment equation. We assumed money wage rate rigidity in the analysis of growth cycle(Chapter 3). In this chapter we will assume money wage rate flexibility in the sense to be explained shortly. Corresponding to this revision of our premiss we have to reexamine the price adjustment equation. It seems useful in this case to resort to Keynes' fundamental equation of the general price level. It presents the following relationship between the general price level p and the supply price p_S under the assumption that all of the difference between planned investment I and planned saving S is absorbed by windfall prfits or losses;[1]

That is,

$$(4. 1) \quad p = p_S + \frac{I - S}{Y_r}.$$

In other words the price level p is equal to the supply price p_S (i.e., the sum of wage earnings and the short run normal profits per unit of output) plus windfall profits or losses per unit of output. This fundamental equation is nothing

---

1) J. M. Keynes: Treatise on Money, vol. 1, 1930, pp. 135-140.

but an identity obtained under the above assumption.

The excess demand and supply of output is assumed in this fundamental equation to be absorbed entirely by immediate changes in prices and not in output. Even if excess demand and supply tended to disappear through changes in prices as the traditional micro-analysis propounds, it would not be reflected in immediate price changes as the process would take some time. In addition, excess demand or supply would, to some extent, be adjusted initially by changes in product inventories and/or backlogs of orders and by firms' production response, so that it will not be absorbed entirely by changes in prices. It is for these reasons that Keynes had to abandon the fundamental equation, and had to turn to the theory of the investment-multiplier. The theory made it clear that excess demand or supply leads to output changes as well as price changes with the former type of adjustment playing an important role in the case of under employment. When we take into account the existence of such adjustment processes concerning excess demand or supply, we should modify the second term of the right-hand side of the Keynesian fundamental equation. In addition, we must conceive of the price adjustment equation in terms of a dynamic process of adjustment. We might consider in this case that the difference between the price level p and the supply price p_s, i.e., windfall profits or losses per unit of output reacts dynamically to excess demand. It is not essentially different from supposing that the ratio of prices to the supply price (p/p_s) responds dynamically to the excess output demand. Therefore, let us formulate the price adjustment process in the form that the proportional rate of growth of (p/p_s) is a function of the ratio of real excess demand to capital stock, $(I_r - S_r)/K$. Denoting the rate of growth of supply price by π_s, we obtain[2]

---

2) In our analysis of growth cycle we expressed the E function in the form of $E[\int_{-\infty}^{t}(\frac{I_r}{K} - s\frac{y}{k})d\tau]$. We used it to analyze employment inflation in the early stage of our study. But it became evident that to use it makes the analysis difficult mathematically. Therefore we assume such a simple E

$$(4.\ 2) \quad \pi = E\left[\ \frac{I_r}{K} - s\ \frac{y}{k}\ \right] + \pi_s, \quad E' > 0, \quad E(0) = 0.$$

When expressing the short run rate of normal profits by ρ, money wage rate per unit of effective labor by w, labor productivity with respect to effective labor by y, the supply price p_s is given by

$$(4.\ 3) \quad p_s = (1 + \rho)\ \frac{w}{y}.$$

In the following analysis we shall assume that ρ is constant through time. Then we can obtain from equation (4. 3)

$$(4.\ 4) \quad \pi_s = \omega - \frac{\dot{y}}{y},$$

where ω is the proportional rate of growth of money wage rate.

2. Wage Adjustment Equation

Next let us examine the adjustment equation of money wage rate. We are concerned here with the process of adjustment of demand and supply in the labor market, in regard to which we will investigate the Phillips curve. It is assumed that the rate of change in money wage rate ω depends upon the excess demand for labor. The unemployment rate is employed in the Phillips curve as an index of the excess supply of labor.[3]

There exists a crucial problem in this examination. Namely, the unemployment

---

function as equation (4. 2) to simplify our analysis. We express our thanks for K. Kuga and S. Onari's comments on our early draft.

3) A. W. Phillips: The Relation between Unemployment and the Rate of Change of Money Wage Rates in the United Kingdom, 1861-1957, Economica, Nov. 1958, pp. 283-299. See also R. G. Lipsey: The Relation between Unemployment and the Rate of Change of Money Wage Rates in the United Kingdom, 1861-1952: A Further Analysis, Economica, Feb. 1960, pp. 1-31, E. A. Kuska: The Simple Analytics of the Phillips Curve, Economica, Nov. 1966, pp. 462-467.

rate is an _ex-post_ magnitude, but the excess demand for labor is an _ex-ante_ one, and their correspondence is not necessarily one-to-one, because the unemployment rate should be zero or positive even if the demand for labor is one and half times or twice as much as the supply of labor. When there is an excess demand for labor, on one hand there is a certain response in the rate of change of wage rate and on the other hand employment is determined at a certain level, which, in conjunction with the existing amount of labor, determines the unemployment rate. The difficulty with the usual Phillips curve interpretation is the implicit simultaneous connection between the unemployment rate and the rate of change in money wage rates in the sense that both of these arise from the fundamental excess demand for labor.

It seems more appropriate to relate ω with the excess demand for labor itself, apart from the Phillips curve which connects ω with the unemployment rate. An important empirical problem has to be resolved, i.e. how do we express excess demand for labor in terms of an observable variable ?. We will not deal with this problem here.[4] Although there exist buffer stocks of products and/or orders backlog possibilities to accomodate excess demand (supply) for output, no such possibilities exist in the case of labor market adjustments. Therefore we may suppose, as the traditional theory of price asserts, that the excess demand for labor is reflected in wage rate changes, while on the other hand, excess demand for output is reflected initially on output adjustment rather than on price adjustment. Now we must ask ourselves if it is suitable to relate the rate of change of the money wage rate directly to the demand-supply ratio of labor ? It seems necessary at this point that we investigate the behavior underlying labor supply.

---

4) There are available figures concerning both the number of applicants for employment and that of offered vacancies for employment reported by the Employment Agency in Japan. We are able to get an _ex-ante_ proxy to represent the ratio of demand to supply of labor by means of the ratio of the number of offered vacanies for employment to that of applicants for employment. A. Ono's study of the wage adjustment function is a pioneer's work using (the reciprocal of) this ratio. See A. Ono: Wages Dynamics in Post-War Japan(in Japanese), _Economic Studies Quarterly_ vol. 16, Nov. 1955, pp. 17-28.

It is traditionally assumed that the supply of labor is an increasing function
of either the money or the real wage rate in its simplest form. It seems, however, that where labor productivity differs, labor supply will differ at any given
money or real wage rate. That is, generally speaking, more labor will be supplied
in the situation having lower productivity than otherwise, assuming the same rate
of money or real wages. This suggests that laborers have wage rates which they
judge to be reasonable and that the supply of labor will increase if the market
rate of wages rises above the subjective rate and decrease in the case where the
market rate is lower. (Incidentally there will be the possibility that the supply
of labor is diminished when market wage rates rise above the subjective rate. We
shall refer to it later.) We can easily formalize this.

   Let us denote the market money wage rate per unit of physical labor by $\bar{w}$,
the subjective rate of money wage per unit of physical labor, which an individual
deems to be reasonable for his labor, by $\bar{w}_R$. We shall call $\bar{w}_R$ the required wage.
When we express his physical hours available for employment by $\bar{N}$, and his physical
labor supply by $\bar{N}_S$, the difference $(\bar{N} - \bar{N}_S)$ represents hours available for his
leisure. We shall assume that the individual decides on the following independ-
ently: (1) whether he supplies his labor or chooses leisure under a given amount
of $\bar{N}$, (2) whether he consumes or saves a fixed income obtained from his labor
supply or other sources, and (3) in which types of assets he holds his savings.
We are concerned here with the decision at the first stage. We may suppose that
the individual takes into consideration real income obtained from his labor supply $(\overline{wN}/p)$ as well as real income subjectively evaluated against hours withheld
for leisure $[\bar{w}_R(\bar{N} - \bar{N}_S)/p]$ to decide his amount of labor supply, and accordingly
his hours for leisure. That is, let

$$(4.\ 5)\quad U = V[\ \frac{\bar{w}}{p}\ \bar{N}_S,\ \frac{\bar{w}_R}{p}\ (\bar{N} - \bar{N}_S)\ ],\qquad V_1 > 0,\qquad V_2 > 0$$

be his utility function, and assume that he determines his amount of labor supply

$\overline{N}_S$ so that he may maximize his utility. From the necessary condition for a maximum of U with respect to $\overline{N}_S$ we obtain

(4. 6) $\overline{N} = \overline{N}(\overline{w}, \overline{w}_R, p, \overline{N})$.

When we assume diminishing marginal utilities of income and leisure, V_{11} and V_{22} are negative, respectively. On the other hand, we may suppose $V_{12} > 0$, because pleasure obtained from leisure will increase with a concomitant increase in income actually earned. Thus the second order condition for a maximum is satisfied. And under these conditions the labor supply $\overline{N}_S$ will increase when the hours available for labor $\overline{N}$ increases.[5]

What are the reactions of labor supply to changes in the money wage rate $\overline{w}$ and the required wage rate $\overline{w}_R$? Let us assume for simplicity that the utility function (4. 5) is linear homogeneous with respect to actual income and real income subjectively evaluated against leisure-time. Then the utility function will have the following form

(4. 7) $U = \dfrac{\overline{w}_R}{p} \cdot V[\ \dfrac{\overline{w}}{\overline{w}_R}\ \overline{N}_S,\ 1 - \overline{N}_S\ ]$,

---

5) The second order condition for a maximum is

$$V_{11}(\overline{w}/p)^2 - 2V_{12}(\overline{w}_R/p) + V_{22}(\overline{w}_R/p)^2 < 0,$$

and it is satisfied if $V_{11} < 0$, $V_{22} < 0$, and $V_{12} > 0$. On the other hand, we get the following relationship from the necessary condition $V_1(\overline{w}/p) - V_2(\overline{w}_R/p) = 0$:

$$\frac{d\overline{N}_S}{d\overline{N}} = \frac{- V_{12}(\overline{w}/p)(\overline{w}_R/p) + V_{22}(\overline{w}_R/p)^2}{V_{11}(\overline{w}/p)^2 - 2V_{12}(\overline{w}/p)(\overline{w}_R/p) + V_{22}(\overline{w}_R/p)^2}.$$

This is positive under the above conditions.

where we choose our unit of measure such that the available physical hours $\bar{N}$ will be equal to unity and $\bar{N}_S$ refers to the proportion of labor supply to the available physical hours. We obtain in this case

$$(4.8) \quad \frac{d\bar{N}_S}{d(\bar{w}/\bar{w}_R)} = \frac{-V_1(1 - R_R) + V_{12}\bar{N}_S}{V_{11}(\bar{w}/\bar{w}_R)^2 - 2V_{12}(\bar{w}/\bar{w}_R) + V_{22}}$$

from the necessary condition for a maximum, where

$$(4.9) \quad R_R \equiv - \frac{U_{11}}{U_1}\frac{\bar{w}}{\bar{w}_R}\bar{N}_S = - \frac{V_{11}}{V_1}\frac{\bar{w}}{\bar{w}_R}\bar{N}_S.$$

(4.9) is nothing but the degree of relative risk aversion with respect to real income in terms of the required wage unit.

If the relative risk aversion is an increasing function of wealth, then the wealth elasticity of demand for money should be greater than unity as shown by K. Arrow.[6] And with reliance on estimates of wealth or income elasticity of demand for money obtained by M. Friedman and so forth, as well as on the observed secular constancy or rise in the ratio of money held to income or wealth, he proposes to adopt the hypothesis of increasing relative risk aversion.[7] According to our investigation on cross-section data of consumers' assets, however, the income elasticity of demand for money is nearly equal to unity, and the financial wealth elasticity is less than unity.[8] We shall attempt in the next chapter to

---

6) K. Arrow: Essays in the Theory of Risk-Bearing, 1971, p. 103 & pp. 119-120.

7) K. Arrow: Ibid. p. 103. Arrow's hypothesis also depends on his theoretical consideration that "if the utility function is to remain bounded as wealth becomes infinite, then the relative risk aversion cannot tend to a limit below one; similarly, for the utility function to be bounded (from below) as wealth approaches zero, the relative risk aversion cannot approach a limit above one as wealth tends to zero." (Ibid. p. 97).

8) S. Fujino: The Demand for Money of the Household(in Japanese), Economic Review, Vol. 17, Jan. 1966, pp. 37-53. S. Fujino: A Hypothesis of Demands for Financial Assets, Structure of Wealth (in Japanese), edited by S. Fujino, 1969, ch. 6.

resolve the discrepancy between the observed secular rise in the ratio of money held to income or wealth and the cross-section observation by assuming the hypothesis of diminishing relative risk aversion. Based on that up-coming analysis, we shall suppose here that relative risk aversion is a decreasing function of real income. The magnitude of R_R is, we assume, smaller in the economy with high income than in the economy with low income in terms of the required wage unit.

Now, because the denominator of the right-hand side of equation (4. 8) is negative, we can obtain, if the numerator is also negative, a proposition that the supply of labor increases with the rise in the relative wage rate $(\overline{w}/\overline{w}_R)$, which is plausible under the usual conditions. In order for this proposition to be true, R_R must satisfy the following condition: $1 - (V_{12}/V_1)\overline{N}_S > R_R$. Since R_R is positive, we must have $(V_{12}/V_1)\overline{N}_S < 1$ in order to obtain this condition. This condition would not prevail, under our assumption of diminishing relative risk aversion, if the required wage rate $\overline{w}_R$ is higher than the money wage rate $\overline{w}$, so that actual income in terms of the required wage rate is low. Generally speaking, the required wage rate, and therefore, the subjective evaluation of leisure will be high under a high level of real income per head. Thus, it seems that the labor supply would react weakly to changes in the relative wage rate in an economy with high subjevtive evaluation of leisure. Accordingly let us suppose that $d\overline{N}_S/d(\overline{w}/\overline{w}_R)$ is usually positive but it could be zero in the matured economy. In addition to this, $d\overline{N}_S/d(\overline{w}/\overline{w}_R)$ should be zero when available labor-time is fully supplied.

Now let us return to the original definitions of $\overline{N}$ and $\overline{N}_S$. Because $\overline{N}$ is an increasing function of time t in the economy as a whole, depending on the above examination, we may express equation (4. 6) by

$$(4.\ 10)\quad \overline{N}_S = \overline{N}_S(\frac{w}{w_R},\ t),\quad \overline{N}_{S_1} \geqq 0,\quad \overline{N}_{S_2} > 0,$$

where w_R is the required wage rate with regard to labor in terms of efficiency unit, and $w/w_R = \overline{w}/\overline{w}_R$. In some cases $\overline{N}_{S_1}$ will be zero. Note that it has two different meanings.[9]

We may suppose that the market wage rate will change around the level of the required wage rate in the adjustment process of the labor market, if the labor supply behaves in accordance with equation (4. 10). This will occur even if the labor market is competitive. And the more remote is the market from competitive conditions, the more the tendency appears. Thus we shall suppose that the rate of growth of (w/w_R), which will be expressed by $(\omega - \omega_R)$, reacts to the supply-demand ratio of labor (N_S/N_D), and we obtain the following wage rate adjustment equation:

(4. 11) $\omega = W(u) + \omega_R,$ $W' \leqq 0,$

where u indicates the ratio (N_S/N_D), and we define full employment by u = 1. Rigidity of the money wage rate will be expressed by means of W = 0.

According to the traditional theory, the money wage rate reacts flexibly to any value of u, and W(1) is equal to zero. Then, the function W will be repre-

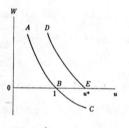

Fig. 4-1

sented, for example, by the curve ABC in Fig. 4-1. On the other hand, if the money wage rate is rigid as far as u > 1 and is flexible as far as u < 1, i.e., it behaves asymmetrically before and after full employment, the function W will be expressed by the curve AB and the horizontal axis to the right of B.

---

9) Because of the two different meanings of $\bar{N}_{S_1} = 0$, the labor supply curve will take such a form as shown in the figure. That is, $\bar{N}_{S_1}$ is zero in the left-hand side from A because of large $R_R^{S_1}$ brought about by a high value of w_R. On the other hand, it is zero in the right-hand side from B because of physical restriction. M. Umemura makes clear that it is important to distinguish between the permanent labor force, which earns the major part of the household sector's income, and the temporary labor force, which gets subsidiary income. Although such distinction does not always correspond to the situation supposed in the text, it is possible that the permanent labor supply is an increasing function of (w/w_R), but the temporary labor supply a decreasing function. See M. Umemura: The Structure of Labor Force and the Problem of Employment (in Japanese), 1971, pp. 1-21, esp. pp. 12-21.

Flexibility of the money wage rate will, however, be restored in the real world at a value of u greater than unity before full employment is reached. The reason is that when the economy nears full employment, excess demand in part of the labor market will cause some wage rate to rise, while wage rates will be rigid in other parts of the labor market where excess supply exists. Labor union activities will intensify the restoration of money wage rate flexibility. If that happens, the function W will be represented, for instance, by the DE curve and the horizontal axis to the right of E in Fig. 4-1. In the following analysis, we shall confine ourselves to investigations in the interval of $u < u^*$, where W' is less than zero.[10]

Now, it seems possible to suppose various alternative hypotheses about variables which will affect the behavior of the required wage rate with respect to natural labor, $\bar{w}_R$.[11] But we shall assume here that the required wage rate is an increasing function of the price level p and labor productivity with respect to natural labor $\bar{y}$, respectively.

$$(4.\ 12) \quad \bar{w}_R = \bar{w}_R(p, \bar{y}), \quad \bar{w}_{R_1} > 0, \quad \bar{w}_{R_2} > 0.$$

Therefore

$$(4.\ 13) \quad \bar{\omega}_R = \lambda_1 \pi + \lambda_2 \frac{\dot{\bar{y}}}{\bar{y}},$$

---

10) See Roshin Minami & Konosuke Odaka: <u>Fluctuations of Wages</u> (in Japanese), 1971, Ch. 4, esp. p. 74. They show empirically that the wage adjustment function in pre-war Japan was like the AB curve in Fig. 4-1, but the post-war one has been changed to take a shape such as the DE curve.

11) For example, on driving the Phillips Curve, C. C. Holt employs the concept of aspiration level, and assumes that it is a decreasing function of the unemployed period of the concerned person and furthermore depends on the general wage rate and vacancy in the labor market. The aspiration level of wage does, we think, resemble our required wage rate. See C. C. Holt: Job Search, Phillips' Wage Relation, and Union Influence — Theory and Evidence, <u>Microeconomic Foundations of Employment and Inflation Theory</u>, edited by E. S. Phelps, 1970, pp. 60-63.

where $\bar{\omega}_R$ represents the rate of growth of $\bar{w}_R$, λ_1 the elasticity of $\bar{w}_R$ with respect to p, which is, we assume, less than unity, λ_2 the elasticity of $\bar{w}_R$ in regard to $\bar{y}$. We shall assume, for simplicity, that the supply-side of labor requires a proportional increase of the wage rate with respect to $\bar{y}$, so that λ_2 is equal to unity.[12] Let us thus denote λ_1 by λ, which we will assume to be constant. Then, since we are able to rewrite $\bar{\omega}_R$ by ω_R and $\bar{y}$ by y in equation (4. 13), we obtain

$$(4.\ 14) \qquad \omega_R = \lambda\pi + \frac{\dot{y}}{y}.$$

When we substitute equation (4. 14) into equation (4. 11), we get

$$(4.\ 15) \qquad \omega = W(u) + \lambda\pi + \frac{\dot{y}}{y}.$$

By combining equations (4. 2), (4. 4) and (4. 15), we get

$$(4.\ 16) \qquad \pi = \frac{1}{1-\lambda} E[\frac{I_r}{K} - s\frac{y}{k}] + \frac{1}{1-\lambda} W(u).$$

Furthermore, we obtain the following equation by substituting equation (4. 16) into (4. 15);

$$(4.\ 15') \qquad \omega = \frac{\lambda}{1-\lambda} E[\frac{I_r}{K} - s\frac{y}{k}] + \frac{1}{1-\lambda} W(u) + \frac{\dot{y}}{y}.$$

We can note that in our model of growth cycle in Chapter 3, W(u) was zero because of the assumption of money wage rate rigidity. Therefore the price adjustment equation (3. 25) corresponds to equation (4. 16) with W(u) = 0.

---

12) Actually λ_2 will perhaps be near to unity, but less than unity.

3. The Rate of Growth of Short Run Demand for Labor

Now let us investigate the short run planning of production of firms to derive the rate of growth of short run demand for labor. We have supposed in the analysis of growth cycle in Chapter 3 that the rate of growth of the output-capital ratio (Y_r/K) reacts to excess output demand per unit of capital stock. Likewise, we shall assume here that firms' short run planning of production is determined by the following relationship which is a generalization of equation (3. 23):

$$(4.\ 17) \qquad \frac{d(Y_r/K)}{dt} \ / \ \left(\frac{Y_r}{K} \right) = H\left[\frac{I_r}{K} - s\, \frac{y}{k} \right], \qquad H' > 0, \quad H(0) = 0.$$

Thus, we obtain

$$(4.\ 18) \qquad \frac{\dot{Y}_{rp}}{Y_r} = H\left[\frac{I_r}{K} - s\, \frac{y}{k} \right] + \frac{\dot{K}_p}{K},$$

where $\dot{Y}_r$ and $\dot{K}$ are given the suffix p to indicate that they are planned values. Firms' demand for labor is derived from both their planned production and their production functions

$$(4.\ 19) \qquad Y_r = F(K,\ N),$$

where it is assumed that (4. 19) is linear homogeneous in K and N and is well-behaved like before. Then we get

$$(4.\ 20) \qquad y = y(k).$$

Denoting the elasticity of output Y_r with respect to capital K by ε, we obtain from equation (4. 19)

$$(4.\ 21) \qquad \frac{\dot{Y}_{rp}}{Y_r} = \varepsilon\, \frac{\dot{K}_p}{K} + (1 - \varepsilon)\, \frac{\dot{N}_p}{N},$$

where ε is less than unity and greater than zero, and we shall assume in the following that ε is constant. Substitution of equation (4. 2) into (4. 18) results in

$$(4.\ 22) \qquad \frac{\dot{N}_p}{N} = \frac{1}{1 - \varepsilon}\ H + \frac{\dot{K}_p}{K}.$$

There are two possibilities regarding how firms determine their short run planned production. In the first alternative, firms always determine their level of output as well as the amount of labor input required in terms of their realized capital stock. We have assumed this situation in the analysis of growth cycle and have further assumed that the planned input of labor is always satisfied. Therefore firms' planned level of output is always realized in the short run. However, firms' planned input of labor is not always realized under flexible money wage rate. The second possibility is that firms take into account both the rate of change in planned output and the rate of change in planned capital stock to determine (the rate of change in) planned input of labor in their short run planning process. Under the first alternative the second term of the right-hand side of equation (4. 22), $\dot{K}_p/K$, is identified with the actual rate of capital accumulation $\dot{K}/K$, and under the second alternative it is equal to I_r/K.

The planned increment in capital stock $\dot{K}_p$ is measured by the difference between the planned and the actual value of capital, so that it is equal to I_r. Similarly the planned increment in labor input $\dot{N}_p$ is measured as the difference between the planned and the actual value of labor input. Therefore it does not equal the increment of demand for labor from one period to the next. Namely, when we express the demand for labor in terms of efficiency unit by N_D, we get $\dot{N}_p \neq \dot{N}_D$ in general. We may assume, however, $\dot{N}_p/N = \dot{N}_D/N_D$.

Now, if there is a gap between planned real investment and planned real saving, how much investment (= saving) is realized will depend on what kind of adjustment is taking place under the gap. If it is fully absorbed by changes in product inventories and/or outstanding orders, then the realized saving (or investment) will be the planned saving. But if a change in the price level occurs, resulting in windfall profits or losses, and, in addition, the saving ratio of real profits is higher than that of real wages, the actual saving will be equal to the planned investment because of the distribution effect. When both saving-ratios are equal, real saving will not be altered by the change in relative share. Even if prices change in this case, the gap between the planned investment and the planned saving will remain as unsatisfied demand.[13]

---

13) Planned real saving S_r is given by

(1) $S_r = sY_r$.

On the other hand, if the saving-ratios from both profits and wages are assumed to be identical, which we denote by s, actual real saving S_r^a is expressed by

(2) $S_r^a = s(\dfrac{\Pi_n}{p_a} + \dfrac{\Pi_w}{p_a}) + s\,\dfrac{wN}{p_a},$

where p_a is actual prices, Π_n normal profits, and Π_w windfall profits (or losses). Windfall profits are expressed by

(3) $\Pi_w = (p_a - p_S)\,Y_r,$

and the supply price is given by

(4) $p_S = (1 + \rho)w\,\dfrac{N}{Y_r}.$

We substitute equations (3) and (4) into equation (2) to get

(5) $S_r^a = s(Y_r + \dfrac{\Pi_n}{p_a} - \rho\,\dfrac{w}{p_a}\,N).$

$(\rho wN/p_a)$ is nothing but (Π_n/p_a). Therefore we obtain

(6) $S_r^a = sY_r$.

That is, when the saving-ratios from profits and wages are identical, actual real saving is equal to the planned, even if windfall profits appear.

Adjustment between investment and saving has to be investigated in terms of money. Let us assume that planned investment in terms of money I exceeds planned saving in terms of money, and that prices will rise. Then, if there is no distribution effect, planned real saving will not show any change. Therefore (I/p) will eventually equal S_r, i.e., prices p will rise so that real investment becomes equal to planned real saving.

For the purpose of this analysis, we shall assume that planned real saving is always realized. In other words,

$$(4.\ 23) \qquad \frac{\dot{K}}{K} = s\,\frac{y}{k}.$$

Thus, in the first case where firms plan their demand for labor under realized capital stock, $\dot{K}_p/K = \dot{K}/K$ in equation (4. 22) and we get the following equation from equations (4. 22) and (4. 23):

$$(4.\ 24) \qquad \frac{\dot{N}_D}{N_D} = \frac{1}{1-\epsilon}\,H + s\,\frac{y}{k}.$$

On the other hand, in the second case where firms take into consideration their planned rate of capital accumulation to plan their demand for labor, we obtain from equation (4. 22)

$$(4.\ 25) \qquad \frac{\dot{N}_D}{N_D} = \frac{1}{1-\epsilon}\,H + \frac{I_r}{K}.$$

4. Rate of Growth of Labor Supply

Let us investigate the rate of growth of the labor supply. From equation (4. 10) the rate of growth of the natural labor supply is given by

$$(4.\ 26) \qquad \frac{\dot{\overline{N}}_S}{\overline{N}_S} = \delta(\omega - \omega_R) + \frac{\overline{N}_{S_2}}{\overline{N}_S},$$

where δ denotes the elasticity of $\overline{N}_S$ with respect to (w/w_R), and $\overline{N}_{S_2}/\overline{N}_S$ the rate of growth of $\overline{N}_S$ under a given (w/w_R). We add to both sides of equation (4. 26) the rate of growth of labor augmentation reflecting Harrod-neutral technical progress, and denote the sum of it and $(\overline{N}_{S_2}/\overline{N}_S)$ by n. We then get

$$(4.\ 27) \qquad \frac{\dot{N}_S}{N_S} = \delta(\omega - \omega_R) + n.$$

n is nothing but the rate of growth of efficient labor. In following we shall assume that δ and n are given, respectively; and that δ is positive or zero. From equations (4. 11) and (4. 27) we obtain

(4. 28) $\quad \dfrac{\dot{N}_S}{N_S} = \delta W(u) + n.$

5. Model

On the basis of our preliminary studies, let us now construct our model of employment inflation.

Let us first express the rate of growth of the ratio of supply of effective labor to demand for effective labor (u).

(4. 29) $\quad \dfrac{\dot{u}}{u} = \dfrac{\dot{N}_S}{N_S} - \dfrac{\dot{N}_D}{N_D}.$

When firms plan the rate of growth of labor input under the realized rate of capital accumulation, we obtain the following equation by substituting equations (4. 24) and (4. 28) into equation (4. 29);

(4. 30) $\quad \dfrac{\dot{u}}{u} = \delta W(u) + n - \dfrac{1}{1 - \epsilon} H - s \dfrac{y}{k}.$

On the other hand, if they plan this same rate under the planned rate of capital accumulation, we get from equations (4. 25), (4. 28) and (4. 29)

(4. 31) $\quad \dfrac{\dot{u}}{u} = \delta W(u) + n - \dfrac{1}{1 - \epsilon} H - \dfrac{I_r}{K}.$

The rate of growth of the actual degree of capital intensity (k) is given by the difference between realized rate of capital accumulation $\dot{K}/K$ and the realized rate of employment $\dot{N}/N$. We defined full employment by u = 1. And we may define under employment by u > 1 and over employment by u < 1. Let us assume that the demand for labor is realized under the condition of under employment, but on the

other hand, the supply of labor is realized under the condition of over employment. Then, the rate of growth of actual employment is $\dot{N}_D/N_D$ when u is greater
than unity, and it is $\dot{N}_S/N_S$ if u is less than unity. In the case of u = 1, the
actual rate of growth of employment is $\dot{N}_D/N_D$ if u changes from the region of u > 1
to u = 1 or from u = 1 to u > 1, and it is $\dot{N}_S/N_S$ if u changes from u < 1 to u = 1
or from u = 1 to u < 1.

Thus, if u > 1, or if u changes from u > 1 to u = 1 or from u = 1 to u > 1,
we get from equations (4. 23) and (4. 24),

$$(4.\ 32) \qquad \frac{\dot{k}}{k} = \frac{\dot{K}}{K} - \frac{\dot{N}_D}{N_D} = -\frac{1}{1-\varepsilon} H[\frac{I_r}{K} - s\frac{y}{k}],$$

when the demand for labor is planned in conjunction with the realized stock of
capital. And when the demand for labor is adjusted to the planned stock of capital, we obtain from equations (4. 23) and (4. 25)

$$(4.\ 33) \qquad \frac{\dot{k}}{k} = \frac{\dot{K}}{K} - \frac{\dot{N}_D}{N_D} = -[\frac{I_r}{K} - s\frac{y}{k}] - \frac{1}{1-\varepsilon} H[\frac{I_r}{K} - s\frac{y}{k}].$$

On the other hand, if u < 1, or if u varies from u < 1 to u = 1, or from
u = 1 to u < 1, the following equation is obtained due to equations (4. 23) and
(4. 28);

$$(4.\ 34) \qquad \frac{\dot{k}}{k} = \frac{\dot{K}}{K} - \frac{\dot{N}_S}{N_S} = s\frac{y}{k} - \delta W(u) - n.$$

Let us briefly summarize the above analysis. If firms adjust their labor
input to the realized stock of capital in their short run planning of production,
we obtain

$$(4.\ 30) \qquad \frac{\dot{u}}{u} = \delta W(u) + n - \frac{1}{1-\varepsilon} H[\frac{I_r}{K} - s\frac{y}{k}] - s\frac{y}{k},$$

and either

$$(4.32) \quad \frac{\dot{k}}{k} = -\frac{1}{1-\varepsilon} H[\frac{I_r}{K} - s\frac{y}{k}],$$

if $u > 1$ or if u changes from $u > 1$ to $u = 1$ or from $u = 1$ to $u > 1$, or

$$(4.34) \quad \frac{\dot{k}}{k} = s\frac{y}{k} - \delta W(u) - n,$$

if $u < 1$ or if u alters from $u < 1$ to $u = 1$ or from $u = 1$ to $u < 1$. And we suppose that if the system starts with the dynamic equations (4.30) and (4.32) from the region of $u > 1$ initially, and then arrives at $u = 1$, through which it enters the region of $u < 1$, its behavior in $u < 1$ is described by the dynamic equations (4.30) and (4.34), whose initial conditions are given by values of u and k obtained from equations (4.30) and (4.32) at $u = 1$. Similarly, if the system starts with the dynamic equations (4.30) and (4.34) from the region of $u < 1$ and then arrives at $u = 1$, through which it enters the region of $u > 1$, its behavior in $u > 1$ is described by the dynamic equations (4.30) and (4.32), whose initial conditions are given by values of u and k obtained from equations (4.30) and (4.34) at $u = 1$. Of course, when the system starts from $u > 1$ (or $u < 1$) and returns there through $u = 1$, equation (4.32) (or (4.34)) continues to be valid. For the sake of expository simplicity, we will describe that equation (4.32) is valid in the region of $u \geq 1$ and equation (4.34) is valid in the region of $u \leq 1$, with the understanding that both equations (4.32) and (4.34) are not always simultaneously valid at $u = 1$.

On the other hand, if firms adjust their input of labor to their planned stock of capital in their short run planning of production, we obtain

$$(4.31) \quad \frac{\dot{u}}{u} = \delta W(u) + n - \frac{1}{1-\varepsilon} H[\frac{I_r}{K} - s\frac{y}{k}] - \frac{I_r}{K},$$

with,

$$(4.33) \quad \frac{\dot{k}}{k} = -[\frac{I_r}{K} - s\frac{y}{k}] - \frac{1}{1-\varepsilon} H[\frac{I_r}{K} - s\frac{y}{k}]$$

in the region of $u \geq 1$, and

$$(4.\ 34) \quad \frac{\dot{k}}{k} = s\ \frac{y}{k} - \delta W(u) - n$$

in the region of $u \leq 1$.

The first model, which consists of equations (4. 30), (4. 32) or (4. 34), yields similar conclusions as those of the second model composed of equations (4. 31), (4. 33) or (4. 34). Therefore, we will confine our analysis to the first model only.

In order to complete our model, the price adjustment equation (4. 16), the wage adjustment equation (4. 15'), the production function (4. 20), the investment function used in Chapter 3, and the relationship between the expected rate of inflation π_e and the actual rate of inflation π, which is represented in Fig. 2-3, must be included with the above equations. For convenience, let us summarize and renumber our system of equations. Our model consists of

$$(4.\ 35) \quad \frac{\dot{u}}{u} = \delta W(u) + n - \frac{1}{1 - \varepsilon}\ H[\ \frac{I_r}{K} - s\ \frac{y}{k}\ ] - s\ \frac{y}{k},$$

$$(4.\ 36) \quad \frac{\dot{k}}{k} = -\ \frac{1}{1 - \varepsilon}\ H[\ \frac{I_r}{K} - s\ \frac{y}{k}\ ],$$

if $u \geq 1$, or

$$(4.\ 37) \quad \frac{\dot{k}}{k} = s\ \frac{y}{k} - \delta W(u) - n,$$

if $u \leq 1$,

$$(4.\ 38) \quad \pi = \frac{1}{1 - \lambda}\ E[\ \frac{I_r}{K} - s\ \frac{y}{k}\ ] + \frac{1}{1 - \lambda}\ W(u),$$

$$(4.39) \quad \omega = \frac{\lambda}{1 - \lambda} E[\frac{I_r}{K} - s \frac{y}{k}] + \frac{1}{1 - \lambda} W(u) + \frac{\dot{y}}{y},$$

$$(4.40) \quad y = y(k),$$

$$(4.41) \quad \frac{I_r}{K} = \alpha[\frac{G(L_S)}{g[y'/(\theta - \pi_e)]} - 1],$$

and

$$(4.42) \quad \pi_e = \pi_e(\pi).$$

There are seven equations and seven endogenous variables: u, k, y, I_r/K, π, π_e, and ω. In this model we presuppose the short run basic relationships, although investment is not always equal to saving. Therefore firms' subjective rate of discount is assumed to be constant. For simplicity, we shall assume that the expected marginal productivity of capital is always equal to the actual one. Furthermore the ratio of real money supply to capital stock L_S is assumed to be a parameter. We can neglect the rate of interest, which is determined by the short run equilibrium equation of demand for and supply of money, because it has no feedback effect on the other parts of our system.

4.3 Steady State Employment Inflation

Let us proceed to analyze the phenomenon which we call employment inflation. We begin by first distinguishing two phases of the supply of natural labor. In the first phase, the elasticity of the supply of natural labor $\overline{N}_S$ with respect to the relative wage rate (w/w_R) is positive in general, so that the rise in the relative wage rate (w/w_R) will induce an additional supply of labor. In some case, however, it is possible that δ is zero. In the second phase, the existing amount of labor is already fully employed, so that an increase in the relative wage rate (w/w_R) can bring forth no more employment without an expansion of the existing labor. The elasticity δ becomes zero in this phase.

Let us examine the steady state growth in our model. Steady state growth is defined by $u = 0$ and $k = 0$. If the system lies in the region of $u \geq 1$, for steady state growth we require from equation (4. 35)

$$(4. 43) \qquad \frac{1}{1 - \varepsilon} \, H[\, \frac{I_r}{K} - s \, \frac{y}{k} \,] + s \, \frac{y}{k} = \delta W(u) + n,$$

and from equation (4. 36)

$$(4. 44) \qquad \frac{1}{1 - \varepsilon} \, H[\, \frac{I_r}{K} - s \, \frac{y}{k} \,] = 0.$$

Owing to the characteristics of the H function, for (4. 44) to prevail, we must have

$$(4. 45) \qquad \frac{I_r}{K} = s \, \frac{y}{k}.$$

And we derive from equations (4. 43) and (4. 44)

$$(4. 46) \qquad s \, \frac{y}{k} = \delta W(u) + n.$$

On the other hand, if $u \leq 1$, equation (4. 43) is obtained from equation (4. 35), and equation (4. 46) is established directly from equation (4. 37). Therefore, we get equation (4. 44) from equations (4. 43) and (4. 46). In other words, the requirements for steady state are the same for both $u \geq$ and $u \leq 1$.

Thus, if δ is positive in the first phase of employment inflation, under steady state growth for both $u \geq 1$ and $u \leq 1$, we will have the actual rate of capital accumulation (sy/k) greater than the natural rate of growth of labor n, which includes labor augmenting technical progress, and the relative wage rate (w/w_R) will increase to satisfy the gap by making the rate of growth of employment rise above the natural rate of growth of labor. If δ is equal to zero, the rate of

capital accumulation will equal the natural rate of growth. And in any case sav-

ing will be equal to investment by equation (4. 45).[14]

In this steady state, we get from equations (4. 38) and (4. 39)

$$(4.\ 47) \qquad \pi = \omega = \frac{1}{1 - \lambda} \, W(u),$$

i.e., both the actual rate of inflation and the rate of growth of money wage take

a same positive value. Thus, if our system has a tendency to converge to the

steady state, the economy will experience, sooner or later, cumulative increases

in prices and money wage rates. In this case, although the real wage rate of ef-

ficient labor is constant, the rate of growth of the real wage rate of natural

labor will be equal to the rate of technical progress. It should be noted that

this kind of inflation occurs under the condition that the monetary authorities

keep constant the ratio of real supply of money to capital stock L_s.

If δ is greater than zero, we obtain from equations (4. 46) and (4. 47)

$$(4.\ 48) \qquad \pi = \omega = \frac{1}{\delta(1 - \lambda)} \, (s \, \frac{y}{k} - n).$$

On the other hand, if δ is equal to zero and, in addition, the supply-demand ratio

of labor in the steady state is greater than unity, there will appear a situation

that may be termed stagflation. We shall explain this situation in detail later.

---

14) In the steady state in this analysis π_e is not always equal to π. It is assumed, however, that π_e equals π in the long run tendency of monetary growth
which will be analyzed in Chapter 5. The difference shows that of unit-peri-
ods in two systems. If the steady state in this analysis continues for a
sufficiently long duration, we have to consider that the π_e function will
shift so that π_e will be equal to π. In this sense the steady state of this
chapter is more of the short run than in that of Chapter 5.

4. 4   Stability of the First Phase (Case with $\delta > 0$)

Next, let us examine the stability of steady state growth and try to determine whether the system will or will not converge to the situation of employment inflation as mentioned above. We investigate the first phase with $\delta > 0$. For this purpose let us examine how (I_r/K) responds to changes in u and k. We differentiate the investment function (4. 41) with respect to u to get

$$(4. 49) \qquad \frac{\partial(I_r/K)}{\partial u} = - \frac{\alpha G g' y'}{g^2(\theta - \pi_e)^2} \cdot \frac{d\pi_e}{d\pi} \cdot \frac{\partial\pi}{\partial u}.$$

In addition, we obtain from the price adjustment equation (4. 38)

$$(4. 50) \qquad \frac{\partial\pi}{\partial u} = \frac{E'}{1 - \lambda} \cdot \frac{\partial(I_r/K)}{\partial u} + \frac{W'}{1 - \lambda}.$$

Substitution of equation (4. 50) into equation (4. 49) yields

$$(4. 51) \qquad \frac{\partial(I_r/K)}{\partial u} = \frac{- \dfrac{\alpha G g' y' W'}{g^2(\theta - \pi_e)^2(1 - \lambda)} \cdot \dfrac{d\pi_e}{d\pi}}{1 + \dfrac{\alpha G g' y' E'}{g^2(\theta - \pi_e)^2(1 - \lambda)} \cdot \dfrac{d\pi_e}{d\pi}}.$$

Since the situation we are concerned with is located near to the level of full employment, and therefore peaks of growth cycles, we might assume on the basis of the shape of the π_e function that $d\pi_e/d\pi$ is negative.[15] Then we get in the above equation $\partial(I_r/K)/\partial u > 0$.

On the other hand, the effect of k on (I_r/K) is described by

---

15) If $d\pi_e/d\pi$ is positive, the system could be unstable, and employment inflation could be explosive, so that it would be serious.

(4. 52) $\quad \dfrac{\partial(I_r/K)}{\partial k} = -\dfrac{\alpha Gg'}{g^2} \left[\dfrac{y''}{(\theta - \pi_e)} + \dfrac{y'}{(\theta - \pi_e)^2} \cdot \dfrac{d\pi_e}{d\pi} \cdot \dfrac{\partial\pi}{\partial k} \right],$

where

(4. 53) $\quad \dfrac{\partial\pi}{\partial k} = \dfrac{E'}{1 - \lambda} \left[\dfrac{\partial(I_r/K)}{\partial k} - \dfrac{d(sy/k)}{dk} \right],$

so that we get

(4. 54) $\quad \dfrac{\partial(I_r/K)}{\partial k} = \dfrac{-\dfrac{\alpha Gg'}{g^2} \left[\dfrac{y''}{(\theta - \pi_e)} - \dfrac{y'E'}{(\theta-\pi_e)^2(1-\lambda)} \cdot \dfrac{d(sy/k)}{dk} \cdot \dfrac{d\pi_e}{d\pi} \right]}{1 + \dfrac{\alpha Gg'y'E'}{g^2(\theta - \pi_e)^2(1 - \lambda)} \cdot \dfrac{d\pi_e}{d\pi}}.$

We may assume $(\theta - \pi_e) > 0$. Thus, under $d\pi_e/d\pi < 0$, we obtain $\partial(I_r/K)/\partial k < 0$.

With our preliminary analyses completed let us investigate the stability of steady state growth. Differentiation of equation (4. 35) with respect to u yields

(4. 55) $\quad \dfrac{\partial(\dot{u}/u)}{\partial u} = \delta W' - \dfrac{H'}{1 - \varepsilon} \dfrac{\partial(I_r/K)}{\partial u}.$

Since $\delta W'$ is negative, $(H'/1 - \varepsilon)$ is positive and $\partial(I_r/K)/\partial u$ is positive, $\partial(\dot{u}/u)\partial u$ should be negative. Differentiating (4. 43) with respect to k yields

(4. 56) $\quad \dfrac{du}{dk} \bigg|_{\dot{u} = 0} = \dfrac{\dfrac{H'}{1 - \varepsilon} \dfrac{\partial h}{\partial k} + \dfrac{d(sy/k)}{dk}}{\delta W' - \dfrac{H'}{1 - \varepsilon} \cdot \dfrac{\partial(I_r/K)}{\partial u}},$

where $h \equiv I_r/K - sy/k$. The numerator of right-hand side of equation (4. 56) could be positive or negative or zero. However, since the possibility of it being negative is high, we shall assume that it is negative. Thus $du/dk]_{\dot{u}=0} > 0$.

Secondly, if $u \geq 1$, from equation (4. 36) we get

$$(4.\,57) \qquad \frac{\partial(\dot{k}/k)}{\partial k} = - \frac{H'}{1-\varepsilon} \cdot \frac{\partial h}{\partial k}.$$

Although $\partial(I_r/K)/\partial k < 0$ and $d(sy/k)/dk < 0$, we shall suppose that $\partial h/\partial k > 0$.[16] Then, we get $\partial(\dot{k}/k)/\partial k < 0$. And, we have, in the case of the $\dot{k} = 0$ curve,

$$(4.\,58) \qquad \frac{du}{dk}\bigg|_{\substack{\dot{k}=0 \\ u \geq 1}} = \frac{-\,\partial h/\partial k}{\dfrac{\partial(I_r/K)}{\partial u}}.$$

This should be negative.

Thirdly, if $u \leq 1$, from equation (4. 37) we get

$$(4.\,59) \qquad \frac{\partial(\dot{k}/k)}{\partial k} = \frac{d(sy/k)}{dk} < 0,$$

and

$$(4.\,60) \qquad \frac{du}{dk}\bigg|_{\substack{\dot{k}=0 \\ u \leq 1}} = \frac{\dfrac{d(sy/k)}{dk}}{\delta W'} > 0.$$

Let us compare the size of $du/dk]_{\substack{\dot{k}=0 \\ u \leq 1}}$ with that of $du/dk]_{\dot{u}=0}$.

Equations (4. 56), (4. 58), (4. 60) yield

$$(4.\,61) \qquad \frac{\dfrac{du}{dk}\bigg|_{\dot{u}=0} - \dfrac{du}{dk}\bigg|_{\substack{\dot{k}=0 \\ u \leq 1}}}{\dfrac{du}{dk}\bigg|_{\dot{u}=0} - \dfrac{du}{dk}\bigg|_{\substack{\dot{k}=0 \\ u \geq 1}}} = \frac{\dfrac{H'}{1-\varepsilon} \cdot \dfrac{\partial(I_r/K)}{\partial u}}{\delta W'}.$$

---

16) This condition corresponds to the stability condition in the ordinary Keynesian model, $dI_r/dY_r < dS_r/dY_r$.

The right-hand side of this equation is negative. Since $du/dk]_{\dot{u}=0} > 0$ and $du/dk]_{\substack{\dot{k}=0 \\ u\geq 1}} < 0$, $(du/dk]_{\dot{u}=0} - \frac{du}{dk}]_{\substack{\dot{k}=0 \\ u\geq 1}})$ is positive. Therefore $(du/dk]_{\dot{u}=0} - du/dk]_{\substack{\dot{k}=0 \\ u\leq 1}})$ should be negative. Thus

$$(4.62) \qquad \frac{du}{dk}\bigg|_{\substack{\dot{k}=0 \\ u\leq 1}} > \frac{du}{dk}\bigg|_{\dot{u}=0} > 0 > \frac{du}{dk}\bigg|_{\substack{\dot{k}=0 \\ u\geq 1}} .$$

It is evident from equations (4. 35), (4. 36), and (4. 37) that when the $\dot{u} = 0$ curve intersects with the $[\dot{k} = 0]_{u\geq 1}$ curve in the u – k plane, where u > 1, the extended line of $[\dot{k} = 0]_{u\leq 1}$ in the region of u > 1, which would be obtained if $[\dot{k} = 0]_{u\leq 1}$ curve were valid in the region of u > 1, passes through the point of intersection. Similarly, when $\dot{u} = 0$ curve intersects with $[\dot{k} = 0]_{u\leq 1}$ curve in the u – k plane where u < 1, the extended line of $[\dot{k} = 0]_{u\geq 1}$ curve passes through the point of intersection. Furthermore, when any two curves among $\dot{u} = 0$ curve, $[\dot{k} = 0]_{u\leq 1}$ curve and its extended line, and $[\dot{k} = 0]_{u\geq 1}$ curve and its extended line intersect at u = 1, the remainder also passes through the point of intersection. Thus we obtain Fig. 4-2. In Fig. 4-2 the system is globally stable, and steady growth will be established in u > 1 in case (1), in u = 1 in case (2) and u < 1

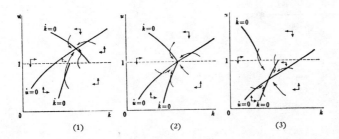

(1) (2) (3)

Fig. 4-2

in case (3).[17]

---

17) It is obvious at once from the figure that case (2) and case (3) are globally
stable. Regarding case (1) we can apply C. Olech's Theorem about the global
stability of dynamic models. In case (1) we obtain

$$\frac{\partial(\dot{u}/u)}{\partial u} < 0, \quad \frac{\partial(\dot{u}/u)}{\partial k} = - \frac{H'}{1-\varepsilon}\frac{\partial h}{\partial k} - \frac{d(sy/k)}{dk} > 0,$$

$$\frac{\partial(\dot{k}/k)}{\partial u} = \frac{H'}{1-\varepsilon}\frac{\partial h}{\partial k} < 0, \quad \frac{\partial(\dot{k}/k)}{\partial k} < 0.$$

Therefore

$$\frac{\partial(\dot{u}/u)}{\partial u} + \frac{\partial(\dot{k}/k)}{\partial k} < 0,$$

$$\frac{\partial(\dot{u}/u)}{\partial u} \cdot \frac{\partial(\dot{k}/k)}{\partial k} - \frac{\partial(\dot{u}/u)}{\partial k} \cdot \frac{\partial(\dot{k}/k)}{\partial u} > 0,$$

and

$$\frac{\partial(\dot{u}/u)}{\partial u} \cdot \frac{\partial(\dot{k}/k)}{\partial k} \neq 0,$$

$$\frac{\partial(\dot{u}/u)}{\partial k} \cdot \frac{\partial(\dot{k}/k)}{\partial u} \neq 0.$$

Thus case (1) is globally stable by Olech's Theorem. See C. Olech: On the
Stability of an Autonomous System in a Plane, Contributions to Differential
Equations, Vol. 1, 1963, pp. 389-400. See also G. Garcia: Olech's Theorem
and the Dynamic Stability of Theories of the Rate of Interest, Journal of
Economic Theory, Vol. 4, June 1972, pp. 541-544.

But steady state growth will not be able to continue permanently. For it is not possible for the rate of growth of employment, which is equal to the rate of accumulation in the steady state, will continue to be above the natural rate of growth of labor by means of the rising relative wage rate. That is, when δ is positive, employment will sooner or later hit the ceiling of the existing labor force since the rate of growth of employment is greater than the natural rate of growth of labor. When this occurs, the rate of growth of employment cannot exceed n. The elasticity of labor supply, δ, becomes zero and employment inflation enters into the second phase. The situation in the second phase is formally similar to that of the first phase where δ = 0. Accordingly, we shall analyze the stability of the second phase as well as of the first phase where δ = 0.

Before we proceed, however, let us investigate the effects of changes in n, s and I_S on steady state growth. We do so in terms of equations (4. 45) and (4. 46). When the natural rate of growth of labor is changed, we get

$$(4.\ 63) \qquad \frac{dk}{dn} = \frac{1}{\Delta} \cdot \frac{\partial(I_r/K)}{\partial u},$$

and

$$(4.\ 64) \qquad \frac{du}{dn} = \frac{-1}{\Delta} \cdot \frac{\partial h}{\partial k},$$

where

$$(4.\ 65) \qquad \Delta \equiv \frac{d(sy/k)}{dk} \cdot \frac{\partial(I_r/K)}{\partial u} + \delta W' \frac{\partial h}{\partial k} < 0.$$

Therefore, dk/dn < 0, du/dn > 0. Next, when the saving ratio s is changed,

$$(4.\ 66) \qquad \frac{dk}{ds} = \frac{-1}{\Delta} \cdot \frac{y}{k} \left[\frac{\partial(I_r/K)}{\partial u} - \delta W' \right],$$

and

$$(4.67) \quad \frac{du}{ds} = \frac{1}{\Delta} \cdot \frac{y}{k} \left[\frac{d(sy/k)}{dk} - \frac{\partial h}{\partial k} \right].$$

Thus we get $dk/ds > 0$ and $du/ds > 0$.

Furthermore, if the ratio of real money supply to capital stock L_S changes, we obtain

$$(4.68) \quad \frac{dk}{dL_S} = \frac{-1}{\Delta} \delta W' \cdot \frac{\partial(I_r/K)}{\partial L_S},$$

and

$$(4.69) \quad \frac{du}{dL_S} = \frac{-1}{\Delta} \cdot \frac{d(sy/k)}{dk} \cdot \frac{\partial(I_r/K)}{\partial L_S},$$

so that $dk/dL_S < 0$ and $du/dL_S < 0$.

4.5 Stability of the First Phase where $\delta = 0$ and Second Phase

How will our model behave, when the elasticity of labor supply δ is zero because either the relative wage rate is sufficiently low or because of the physical restriction of labor supply ? The former situation will perhaps occur in the first phase of employment inflation in a matured economy, and the latter is nothing but the second phase of employment inflation. Let us examine the model's steady state growth stability properties. From equation (4.35) we obtain

$$(4.70) \quad \frac{\partial(\dot{u}/u)}{\partial u} = - \frac{H'}{1 - \varepsilon} \cdot \frac{\partial(I_r/K)}{\partial u} < 0,$$

and

$$(4.\ 71) \quad \frac{du}{dk}\bigg|_{\dot{u}=0} = \frac{\dfrac{H'}{1-\varepsilon} \cdot \dfrac{\partial h}{\partial k} + \dfrac{d(sy/k)}{dk}}{-\dfrac{H'}{1-\varepsilon} \cdot \dfrac{\partial (I_r/K)}{\partial u}} > 0.$$

Next, in the region of $u \geq 1$ we obtain from equation $(4.\ 36)$

$$(4.\ 72) \quad \frac{\partial (\dot{k}/k)}{\partial k} = -\frac{H'}{1-\varepsilon} \cdot \frac{\partial h}{\partial k} < 0,$$

and

$$(4.\ 73) \quad \frac{du}{dk}\bigg|_{\substack{\dot{k}=0 \\ u \geq 1}} = \frac{\dfrac{\partial h}{\partial k}}{-\dfrac{\partial (I_r/K)}{\partial u}} < 0.$$

It is evident from equations $(4.\ 71)$ and $(4.\ 73)$ that

$$(4.\ 74) \quad \frac{du}{dk}\bigg|_{\substack{\dot{k}=0 \\ u \geq 1}} < \frac{du}{dk}\bigg|_{\dot{u}=0}.$$

Furthermore, in the region of $u \leq 1$ we get from equation $(4.\ 37)$

$$(4.\ 75) \quad \frac{\partial (\dot{k}/k)}{\partial k} = \frac{d(sy/k)}{dk} < 0.$$

The $\dot{k} = 0$ curve is independent of u.

We get Fig. 4-3 in this case, where the system is globally stable (Olech's Theorem is statisfied in all cases).

Under steady state growth, the following relations are established:

(4. 76) $\quad s \dfrac{y}{k} = n,$

and

(4. 77) $\quad \dfrac{I_r}{K} = s \dfrac{y}{k}.$

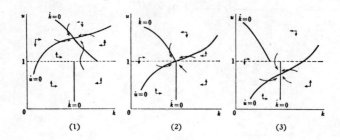

Fig. 4-3

The steady state values of k and u are influenced by the changes in n, s and L_S as follows;

(4. 78) $\quad \dfrac{dk}{dn} = \dfrac{1}{\dfrac{d(sy/k)}{dk}} < 0,$

(4. 79) $\quad \dfrac{du}{dn} = \dfrac{-\dfrac{\partial h}{\partial k}}{\dfrac{d(sy/k)}{dk} \cdot \dfrac{\partial(I_r/K)}{\partial u}} > 0,$

(4. 80) $\quad \dfrac{dk}{ds} = \dfrac{-y/k}{\dfrac{d(sy/k)}{dk}} > 0,$

$$(4.\ 81) \quad \frac{du}{ds} = \frac{\dfrac{y}{k} \cdot \dfrac{\partial(I_r/K)}{\partial k}}{\dfrac{d(sy/k)}{dk} \cdot \dfrac{\partial(I_r/K)}{\partial u}} > 0,$$

$$(4.\ 82) \quad \frac{dk}{dL_S} = 0,$$

and

$$(4.\ 83) \quad \frac{du}{dL_S} = \frac{-\dfrac{\partial(I_r/K)}{\partial L_S}}{\dfrac{\partial(I_r/K)}{\partial u}} < 0.$$

Now, if case (1) of Fig. 4-3 were to appear in the first phase of employment inflation in a matured economy because of the weak response of the labor supply to changes in the relative wage rate, the system will converge to a steady state with $u > 1$. And the rate of growth of employment will equal the natural rate of growth of labor, so that there will be a coexistence of inflation and unemployment in the system. This is nothing but stagflation. In case (2) of Fig. 4-3, the system experiences inflation under full employment. But this will occur just by chance. And in regard to case (3) of Fig. 4-3, the system will converge to a steady state with over employment and sustained inflation.

4. 6   Employment Inflation and Economic Policy

In the first and second phases of employment inflation as analyzed above, we cannot avoid inflation if we attempt to attain full employment, i.e., $u = 1$. We can consider positive saving brought about by means of taxation and the ratio of real stock of money to capital stock L_S as instruments to achieve full employment in our model. The former has not yet been explicitly incorporated into our model. Positive saving of the government will be brought about by taxation without corresponding expenditures. Since the imposition of taxes on firms will complicate matters, let us consider household income taxation. If the government imposes proportional income tax, the rate of which is t_a, the ratio of households' saving to capital stock will be $[s(1 - t_a)(y/k)]$. Suppose the decrease in money stock brought about by the taxation is counterbalanced by the government's purchase of securities issued by firms. In addition let us assume that interest revenue obtained by the government, owing to its holdings of securities, is transfered to households by means of reducing the tax rate. Then the ratio of government's saving to capital stock is $t_a.(y/k)$. Therefore the ratio of saving as a whole to capital stock is $[s + t_a(1 - s)](y/k)$. Let us denote the saving ratio $[s + t_a(1 - s)]$ by $\bar{s}$, which corresponds to the s we have been using so far. And, if $t_a > 0$, then $\bar{s} > s$.

Now, the steady state growth capital intensity k and supply-demand ratio of labor u are affected by changes in the saving ratio $\bar{s}$ and the ratio of real money stock to capital stock L_S as shown in Table 4-1. Therefore, if we attempt to attain full employment in each phase of employment inflation, our policies should be as follows.

Table 4-1: Effects of Changes in $\bar{s}$ and L_S on Steady State

	$\delta > 0$	$\delta = 0$
$\dfrac{dk}{d\bar{s}}$	+	+
$\dfrac{du}{d\bar{s}}$	+	+
$\dfrac{dk}{dL_S}$	−	0
$\dfrac{du}{dL_S}$	−	−

Since the increase in $\bar{s}$ raises u and the increase in L_S decreases u, we need to decrease $\bar{s}$ by a tax reduction and to increase L_S to attain full employment if the steady state value of u is greater than unity. On the other hand, if u is less than unity in the steady state, we have to raise $\bar{s}$ by a tax increase or reduce L_S.

When the steady state is established at u = 1, inflation will inevitably appear. That is, when we attempt to achieve full employment, inflation will occur. We have to consider such inflation as a cost for maintaining full employment.

Finally, there is one point which should be reiterated. That is, as we have noted in footnote (5), if $d\pi_e/d\pi$ is positive, the system could be unstable. And when the system is undergoing sustained inflation, the π_e function could shift upwards, since it is likely that firms' judgement about the normal rate of inflation will be raised owing to the fact that π is maintained at a high level. The system could then face a situation where $d\pi_e/d\pi > 0$, and therefore could become unstable. In this case it is most likely that the system will experience an explosive type of inflation, and it will be very difficult to combat against such an inflation by means of economic policies. The primary policy objective in this case will be the need to crush inflationary psychology (i.e., forces which tend to raise the normal rate of inflation) by means of a large increase in $\bar{s}$ or a great decrease of L_S in order to shift the π_e function downward. Because we would need a complicated analysis for dealing fully with this problem, we shall abstain from further investigation of this problem.

CHAPTER 5

A NEO-KEYNESIAN THEORY OF MONETARY GROWTH

5.1 Problems

On explaining the process of growth cycle in terms of changes in the expected marginal productivity of capital, we have assumed in Chapter 3 that the cyclical limits of the output-capital ratio are constant over all growth cycles. If
this assumption is true, the ratio would virtually remain constant over a long
period of cyclical economic growth. We face two questions. The first is whether
such a long-run tendency of the output-capital ratio can be observed or not, and
the second is whether we are able to explain the behavior by our theoretical
model of monetary growth. With respect to the first question we shall summarize
our observations in the Japanese economy later. To attack the second question,
we shall refer to, as we have already mentioned in Chapter 2, peaks of growth
cycles where the economy, we shall assume, reaches full employment under a flexible real wage rate. We shall attempt to construct a model which characterizes
the process of monetary growth over cyclical fluctuations.

According to our investigation, in addition to the secular constancy of the
output-capital ratio, we observe the following tendencies of the variables under
consideration:

(1) The real rate of wage, labor productivity and the capital-labor ratio
increase proportionately.

(2) The nominal rate of interest rise and fall around a constant level, having no increasing or decreasing tendency in the long run.

(3) The ratio of real money stock to capital shows a rising tendency.

These behavior patterns should be interpreted by our model. Among them we
are particularly interested in the rising tendency of the money-capital ratio,
which implies the existence of a similar tendency in the money-income ratio

(i.e., the Marshallian k) under the nearly constant output-capital ratio. Does this mean that the income or wealth elasticity of demand for money is greater than unity ? If we simply compared the real stock of money with real income, the estimated elasticity would be larger than unity. This would be true even if we had used the concept of permanent income, because the trend of observed or measured incomes does not seem to be different from that of permanent incomes. Thus M. Friedman's estimation,[1] which shows that the income or wealth elasticity of demand for money is greater than unity, depends on the rising tendency of the Marshallian k.

As we pointed out in Chapter 4, according to our investigation of cross-section data of consumers' assets, however, the income elasticity of demand for money is nearly equal to unity, and the elasticity with respect to the total amount of financial assets is less than unity. Thus, there is at least a superficial gap between the results obtained by the time-series analysis and those of the cross-section analysis. If the elasticity is less than or equal to unity, the relative risk aversion defined by K. J. Arrow should be a decreasing function of wealth or should be constant. However, he asserts that it is an increasing function of wealth.[2]

There is, furthermore, another inconsistency regarding the behavior of the money-capital ratio or money-income ratio. This pertains to the inconsistency between the observed fact and the theoretical conclusion reached in monetary growth models. Studies of monetary growth usually show that the money-capital ratio or money-income ratio is a constant in steady state.

Thus, there are two kinds of inconsistencies related to the actual behavior of the money-capital ratio. We shall attempt to resolve these inconsistencies with the model to follow.

---

1) M. Friedman: The Demand for Money — Some Theoretical and Empirical Results — Journal of Political Economy, Vol. 67, Aug. 1959, pp. 327-351.

2) K. J. Arrow: Essays in the Theory of Risk-Bearing, 1970, pp. 103-104.

5. 2   Model

Our long run basic relationships shown in Chapter 2 were the production function

(5. 1) $y = y(k)$,

the equilibrium equation of money demand and supply

(5. 2) $g[y'/\theta_R(i_R)] + \dfrac{1}{k} \, m^h(i_R, y) = L_S$,

and the equilibrium equation for saving and investment

(5. 3) $\alpha[\, \dfrac{L^f}{g[y'/\theta_R(i_R)]} - 1\,] = s\,\dfrac{y}{k}$.

If the money stock is supplied through deficit expenditures of the government
sector, equation (5. 3) should be revised to

(5. 3') $\alpha[\, \dfrac{L^f}{g[y'/\theta_R(i_R)]} - 1\,] + (\mu - \phi_M)L_S = s\,\dfrac{y}{k}$,

where μ is the rate of growth of $\overline{M}_S$, and ϕ_M is the rate of growth of the monetization shift parameter. But since the revision does not essentially change our
conclusion, we shall confine ourselves to equation (5. 3).

For the sake of simplicity, we assume that m^h is linear homogeneous with
respect to y, so that $(1/k).m^h(i_R, y)$, in equation (5. 2), is replaced by $m^h(i_R,$
$y/k)$. Denote (ϕ_M/ϕ_F) by ϕ, the rate of growth of $\phi(t)$ as ϕ, and the initial value
of a variable by the suffix 0. Rewriting equation (5. 2), we obtain

(5. 2') $g[y'/\theta_R(i_R)] + m^h(i_R, y/k) = \dfrac{\overline{M}_{S_0}}{\phi_0 p_0 K_0} \, e^{(\mu-\phi-\pi-sy/k)t}$.

Representing the left-hand side of equation (5. 2') by $\dot{L}_D$ and differentiating by k yields the following:

$$(5.\ 4) \qquad \frac{\partial L_D}{\partial k} = \frac{g'y''}{\theta_R} + m_2^h \frac{y'k - y}{k^2}.$$

Because the first term of the right-hand side of equation (5. 4) is positive and the second term is negative, we cannot determine the sign of $\partial L_D/\partial k$ unless we know the relative magnitudes. However, it is plausible to suppose that $\partial L_D/\partial(y/k)$ is positive. Under this assumption $\partial L_D/\partial k$ should be negative, since $\partial L_D/\partial(y/k)$ is equal to $\partial L_D/\partial(y/k).d(y/k)/dk$ and $d(y/k)/dk$ is negative. Next, differentiating L_D by i_R, we get

$$(5.\ 5) \qquad \frac{\partial L_D}{\partial i_R} = - g' \frac{y'\theta_R'}{\theta_R^2} + m_1^h.$$

$g'y'\theta_R'/\theta_R^2$ and m_1^h are both negative, but we might assume that the absolute value of the former is less than that of the latter, so that $\partial L_D/\partial i_R$ is negative.

Since we now have three equations (5. 1), (5. 2') and (5. 3), and four endogenous variables y, k, i_R and π, we need one more equation to complete of model. And moreover, it is a dynamic equation that is required to build a growth model. There are three alternatives in this regard. The first is to suppose that the capital-labor ratio k is given at each point of time, being changed from time to time by the accumulation of capital and growth of the labor force. This will be expressed by

$$(5.\ 6) \qquad \frac{\dot{k}}{k} = s \frac{y}{k} - n,$$

where n is the rate of growth of labor in terms of efficiency unit. This is the neo-classical type of dynamic equation. In this neo-classical model the real rate of interest i_R is determined in such a manner that investment will be equal to saving in equation (5. 3) under a given k at full employment and the rate of inflation π is determined so as to satisfy the condition for monetary equilibrium (5. 2').

The second possibility is to assume that the rate of inflation is a dynamic variable in the equation system (5. 2') and (5. 3). The Keynesian system implicitly assumes that quantity adjustment works more quickly than price adjustment in the process of balancing output demand and supply. Following this assumption, we may suppose that the change in the rate of inflation reflects the long run relationship between saving and investment, which could be, we think, expressed by the difference between the investment-capital ratio at each point of time and a given saving-capital ratio. Because investment is equal to saving at each point of time, we can express the above assumption as

$$(5. 7) \quad \dot{\pi} = \alpha [\, s \, \frac{y}{k} - s \, \frac{y^*}{k^*} \,],$$

where α is a positive constant, and y^*/k^* is a given value of the output-capital ratio. Under this dynamic equation we might suppose that (y/k) is the main variable which permits adjustments between investment and saving at each point of time, and i_R, and therefore $(i_R + \pi)$, is primarily for balancing money demand and supply. This is, we may say, nothing but a Keynesian type of growth model.

Finally, it is possible to suppose that the real rate of interest changes in accordance with

$$(5. 8) \quad \dot{i}_R = \beta [\, s \, \frac{y}{k} - s \, \frac{y^*}{k^*} \,],$$

where β is a positive constant. This implies that the long run saving-investment relationship is adjusted by the real rate of interest. Therefore it supposes, we may say, that the neo-classical theory of saving and investment operates in the long run. If we adopt this equation, (y/k) is determined by equation (5. 3), and

π by equation (5. 2'). Thus, this system is a kind of hybrid model of both the first and the second one.

How should we choose among the three alternative dynamic equations ? Our choice must depend on the adjustment speeds of π, i_R, and k(or y/k). We should choose the variable with the slowest adjustment speed as our dynamic one. It seems that the parametric function of the real rate of interest in the saving-investment relationship appears most slowly. Therefore, we might assume equation (5. 8) to be our dynamic equation. We can easily show that the long run steady state properties would be the same, regardless of what dynamic equation we chose. However, the convergence paths would be different among these three equations.[3]

5. 3 Steady State Economic Growth

Let us define the steady state of our model by $\dot{i}_R = 0$. Then we obtain from equation (5. 8)

$$(5. 9) \qquad \frac{y}{k} = \frac{y^*}{k^*} \, .$$

That is, (y/k), therefore, k should be constant. It is clear that

$$(5. 10) \qquad \frac{y}{k} = \frac{n}{s},$$

---

3) A more sophisticated model would be obtained by distinguishing between the short run, the intermediate run and the long run. That is, a multi-dynamic model could be constructed by supposing that the rate of inflation and the long run real rate of interest are given in the short run, where the short run equilibrium values of i_R and (y/k) are determined, that the rate of inflation is changed from short period to short period according to a dynamic equation like (5. 7) and the intermediate run equilibrium is established under a given long run real rate of interest, and that the latter changes dynamically in the long run. This kind of analysis, was attempted elsewhere but is not present here because it is felt that the above hybrid model is sufficient to explain the actual course of economic growth. See S. Fujino: Monetary Growth and Secular Inflation (in Japanese), Economic Review, Vol. 24, July 1973, pp. 231-246.

if k is constant over time. Under our well-behaved production function there exists such a k, which will fix the steady state value of i_R through equation (5. 3), so that the value of π will be determined by equation (5. 2'). The ratio of the real demand for money to capital has to be fixed in steady state. Therefore L_S should be also constant. We thus obtain

(5. 11) $\pi = \mu - \phi - n.$

Formally speaking, if the monetary authorities change the rate of growth of money supply μ, the rate of inflation in the steady state should also be altered by the same magnitude, since we obtain from equation (5. 11)

(5. 12) $\dfrac{d\pi}{d\mu} = 1.$

But i_R and y/k (or k) will maintain their original steady state value. In the conventional study of monetary growth, whether money is neutral or not is defined in terms of whether or not the introduction of money into the economic system affects the steady state value of k.[4] In the static analysis, however, the neutrality of money means that the increase in money stock brings about a proportionate rise in prices without affecting the real variables including the real rate of interest.[5] A dynamic version of the static concept of neutrality of money may be defined in terms of the condition that changes in μ lead to proportionate variation in π with no affect on k and i_R. According to this definition, money is neutral in our model.

---

4)   See J. Tobin: The Neutrality of Money in Growth Models: A Comment, Economica, Feb. 1967, pp. 69-72.

5)   See, for example, D. Patinkin: Money, Interest and Prices, 1965, p. 75.

5. 4 Stability

In order to examine the stability of the steady state, let us first investigate the parametric effects of a change in i_R on k and π in equations (5. 2') and (5. 3). We differentiate these equations with respect to i_R to obtain

(5. 13)
$$
\begin{bmatrix}
(L_{D_1} + stL_S)\dfrac{dz}{dk} & tL_S \\[2em]
(I_1 - s)\dfrac{dz}{dk} & 0
\end{bmatrix}
\begin{bmatrix}
\dfrac{dk}{di_R} \\[2em]
\dfrac{d\pi}{di_R}
\end{bmatrix}
=
\begin{bmatrix}
-L_{D_2} \\[2em]
-I_2\,\theta_R'
\end{bmatrix},
$$

where z denotes (y/k), and I_1 and I_2 express the derivatives of I_r/K with respect to (y/k) and θ_R, respectively. dz/dk and I_2 are negative, and I_1 is positive. Under the Keynesian stability condition, the derivative of investment with respect to output is less than that of saving. In our analysis this condition corresponds to $(I_1 - s) < 0$. Suppose this is satisfied. Then the determinant of the matrix in equation (5. 13) should be positive, because it is equal to $tL_S(s - I_1)$. And we obtain from equation (5. 13)

(5. 14)
$$
\frac{dk}{di_R} = \frac{I_2\,\theta_R'}{(s - I_1)}\frac{dz}{dk} > 0,
$$

(5. 15)
$$
\frac{d\pi}{di_R} = \frac{(I_1 - s)L_{D_2} - I_2\,\theta_R'(L_{D_1} + stL_S)}{tL_S(s - I_1)} > 0.
$$

Thus, when i_R changes in equation (5. 8), we can get

(5. 16)
$$
\frac{\dot{i}_R}{di_R} = \beta s\,\frac{dz}{dk}\frac{dk}{di_R} < 0.
$$

Therefore, steady state economic growth should be stable.

5.5   Implications of Steady State

Let us now turn to some implications of steady state monetary growth. First
of all, labor productivity y and the degree of capital intensity k in terms of
efficient labor will both be constant. Owing to labor augmenting technical progress, however, the labor productivity and the degree of capital intensity in
terms of natural labor will rise, showing parallel movements. As a result, the
output-capital ratio z will remain constant. We think that the labor market is
competitive in the long run. If this is true, the rate of real wage will increase
proportionately with increases in labor productivity. These tendencies correspond
well to observations obtained in the Japanese economy.

Secondly, since the rate of inflation π and the real rate of interest i_R are
constant under steady state monetary growth, the nominal rate of interest should
be constant also.

Thirdly, under steady state the real money-capital ratio, $L_S(= \overline{M}_S/\Phi pK)$, takes
a constant magnitude. As long as the rate of growth of Φ, ϕ, is positive, i.e.,
as long as the rate of growth of the shift parameter of demand function for money
due to monetization is greater than the rate of money augmenting technical progress, however, the actual ratio of real money to capital, $(\overline{M}_S/pK) = \Phi L_S$, will
rise over time. Therefore, we are able to explain the actual process of monetary
growth, because we observe the rising tendency of real money-capital ratio in the
real world.

In addition, we have to notice that this rising tendency will occur in our
model, even if the income elasticity of money is less than unity. Therefore, to
measure the income elasticity of money by means of comparing observed real stock
of money with real income in time series as M. Friedman did is of questionable
usefulness. Taking into consideration estimations using cross-section data, income elasticity of money seems to be less than unity or to be nearly equal to
unity.

Thus, our model of monetary growth can resolve the inconsistencies between the actual time trend of money-capital ratio and the income elasticity of demand for money estimated by cross-section data, and between the former and the theoretical conclusion.

In our discussion so far, we have supposed that the rate of growth of the shift parameter of demand function for money due to monetization is greater than the rate of money augmenting technical progress. It is possible, however, that the former becomes less than the latter in the course of time. We would then expect that the money-capital ratio or money-income ratio will decline over time. The post-war experiences of the U. S. A. and the United Kingdom show declining tendencies in the money-income ratio.[6] In terms of our model, these historical patterns could be interpreted by the assumption that ϕ turned negative in those countries during the post-war period.

Finally, let us examine whether or not the monetary authorities can manipulate the rate of growth of the money stock in order to control the rate of inflation. According to equation (5. 11), it would seem at first glance that the monetary authorities are able to attain any rate of inflation by choosing the magnitude of the rate of growth of money stock, μ under given ϕ and n. However, if the monetary authorities fixed the rate of growth of money stock at a level that is too low to attain full employment, the economy could not sustain it. That is, even if the real rate of wage were flexible, full employment would not be possible under a certain monetary condition, because the rate of money wage is flexible upwards, but not so downwards. Therefore our presupposition that full employment can be attained by the flexibility of real rate of wage implicitly assumes that monetary policy does not prevent the economy from going to full employment, even when the government does not intentionally adopt the full employment policy. Under the full employment policy, which would bring about the

6) See M. Friedman & A. J. Schwartz: A Monetary History of the United States 1867-1960, 1963, ch. 12. D. K. Sheppard: The Growth and Role of UK Financial Institutions 1880-1962, 1971, p. 50.

employment inflation discussed in the previous chapter, the monetary authorities would _afortiori_ be forced to maintain the rate of growth of money supply beyond a certain positive level. And it would seem that in the long run the monetary authorities will have to choose the rate of growth of money supply in the range that

$$(5.\ 17) \qquad \mu \geq \pi_f + \phi + n,$$

where π_f is the rate of inflation at full employment. Thus, the choice of the value of μ would be constrained. And as long as full employment has priority over other policy targets, the optimum long run rate of growth of money supply would be $(\pi_f + \phi + n)$. Therefore, we recommend a monetary policy in which μ is discretionally changed so as to adjust cyclical growth in the short run, but is fixed at $(\pi_f + \mu + n)$ in the long run, even though π_f could be changed.

Vol. 59: J. A. Hanson, Growth in Open Economics. IV, 127 pages. 4°. 1971. DM 16,–

Vol. 60: H. Hauptmann, Schätz- und Kontrolltheorie in stetigen dynamischen Wirtschaftsmodellen. V, 104 Seiten. 4°. 1971. DM 16,–

Vol. 61: K. H. F. Meyer, Wartesysteme mit variabler Bearbeitungsrate. VII, 314 Seiten. 4°. 1971. DM 24,–

Vol. 62: W. Krelle u. G. Gabisch unter Mitarbeit von J. Burgermeister, Wachstumstheorie. VII, 223 Seiten. 4°. 1972. DM 20,–

Vol. 63: J. Kohlas, Monte Carlo Simulation im Operations Research. VI, 162 Seiten. 4°. 1972. DM 16,–

Vol. 64: P. Gessner u. K. Spremann, Optimierung in Funktionenräumen. IV, 120 Seiten. 4°. 1972. DM 16,–

Vol. 65: W. Everling, Exercises in Computer Systems Analysis. VIII, 184 pages. 4°. 1972. DM 18,–

Vol. 66: F. Bauer, P. Garabedian and D. Korn, Supercritical Wing Sections. V, 211 pages. 4°. 1972. DM 20,–

Vol. 67: I. V. Girsanov, Lectures on Mathematical Theory of Extremum Problems. V, 136 pages. 4°. 1972. DM 16,–

Vol. 68: J. Loeckx, Computability and Decidability. An Introduction for Students of Computer Science. VI, 76 pages. 4°. 1972. DM 16,–

Vol. 69: S. Ashour, Sequencing Theory. V, 133 pages. 4°. 1972. DM 16,–

Vol. 70: J. P. Brown, The Economic Effects of Floods. Investigations of a Stochastic Model of Rational Investment Behavior in the Face of Floods. V, 87 pages. 4°. 1972. DM 16,–

Vol. 71: R. Henn und O. Opitz, Konsum- und Produktionstheorie II. V, 134 Seiten. 4°. 1972. DM 16,–

Vol. 72: T. P. Bagchi and J. G. C. Templeton, Numerical Methods in Markov Chains and Bulk Queues. XI, 89 pages. 4°. 1972. DM 16,–

Vol. 73: H. Kiendl, Suboptimale Regler mit abschnittweise linearer Struktur. VI, 146 Seiten. 4°. 1972. DM 16,–

Vol. 74: F. Pokropp, Aggregation von Produktionsfunktionen. VI, 107 Seiten. 4°. 1972. DM 16,–

Vol. 75: GI-Gesellschaft für Informatik e. V. Bericht Nr. 3. 1. Fachtagung über Programmiersprachen · München, 9.–11. März 1971. Herausgegeben im Auftag der Gesellschaft für Informatik von H. Langmaack und M. Paul. VII, 280 Seiten. 4°. 1972. DM 24,–

Vol. 76: G. Fandel, Optimale Entscheidung bei mehrfacher Zielsetzung. 121 Seiten. 4°. 1972. DM 16,–

Vol. 77: A. Auslender, Problemes de Minimax via l'Analyse Convexe et les Inégalités Variationnelles: Théorie et Algorithmes. VII, 132 pages. 4°. 1972. DM 16,–

Vol. 78: GI-Gesellschaft für Informatik e. V. 2. Jahrestagung, Karlsruhe, 2.–4. Oktober 1972. Herausgegeben im Auftrag der Gesellschaft für Informatik von P. Deussen. XI, 576 Seiten. 4°. 1973. DM 36,–

Vol. 79: A. Berman, Cones, Matrices and Mathematical Programming. V, 96 pages. 4°. 1973. DM 16,–

Vol. 80: International Seminar on Trends in Mathematical Modelling, Venice, 13–18 December 1971. Edited by N. Hawkes. VI, 288 pages. 4°. 1973. DM 24,–

Vol. 81: Advanced Course on Software Engineering. Edited by F. L. Bauer. XII, 545 pages. 4°. 1973. DM 32,–

Vol. 82: R. Saeks, Resolution Space, Operators and Systems. X, 267 pages. 4°. 1973. DM 22,–

Vol. 83: NTG/GI-Gesellschaft für Informatik, Nachrichtentechnische Gesellschaft. Fachtagung „Cognitive Verfahren und Systeme", Hamburg, 11.–13. April 1973. Herausgegeben im Auftrag der NTG/GI von Th. Einsele, W. Giloi und H.-H. Nagel. VIII, 373 Seiten. 4°. 1973. DM 28,–

Vol. 84: A. V. Balakrishnan, Stochastic Differential Systems I. Filtering and Control. A Function Space Approach. V, 252 pages. 4°. 1973. DM 22,–

Vol. 85: T. Page, Economics of Involuntary Transfers: A Unified Approach to Pollution and Congestion Externalities. XI, 159 pages. 4°. 1973. DM 18,–

Vol. 86: Symposium on the Theory of Scheduling and Its Applications. Edited by S. E. Elmaghraby. VIII, 437 pages. 4°. 1973. DM 32,–

Vol. 87: G. F. Newell, Approximate Stochastic Behavior of n-Server Service Systems with Large n. VIII, 118 pages. 4°. 1973. DM 16,–

Vol. 88: H. Steckhan, Güterströme in Netzen. VII, 134 Seiten. 4°. 1973. DM 16,–

Vol. 89: J. P. Wallace and A. Sherret, Estimation of Product. Attributes and Their Importances. V, 94 pages. 4°. 1973. DM 16,–

Vol. 90: J.-F. Richard, Posterior and Predictive Densities for Simultaneous Equation Models. VI, 226 pages. 4°. 1973. DM 20,–

Vol. 91: Th. Marschak and R. Selten, General Equilibrium with Price-Making Firms. XI, 246 pages. 4°. 1974. DM 22,–

Vol. 92: E. Dierker, Topological Methods in Walrasian Economics. IV, 130 pages. 4°. 1974. DM 16,–

Vol. 93: 4th IFAC/IFIP International Conference on Digital Computer Applications to Process Control, Zürich/Switzerland, March 19–22, 1974. Edited by M. Mansour and W. Schaufelberger. XVIII, 544 pages. 4°. 1974. DM 36,–

Vol. 94: 4th IFAC/IFIP International Conference on Digital Computer Applications to Process Control, Zürich/Switzerland, March 19–22, 1974. Edited by M. Mansour and W. Schaufelberger. XVIII, 546 pages. 4°. 1974. DM 36,–

Vol. 95: M. Zeleny, Linear Multiobjective Programming. XII, 220 pages. 4°. 1974. DM 20,–

Vol. 96: O. Moeschlin, Zur Theorie von Neumannscher Wachstumsmodelle. XI, 115 Seiten. 4°. 1974. DM 16,–

Vol. 97: G. Schmidt, Über die Stabilität des einfachen Bedienungskanals. VII, 147 Seiten. 4°. 1974. DM 16,–

Vol. 98: Mathematical Methods in Queueing Theory. Proceedings of a Conference at Western Michigan University, May 10–12, 1973. Edited by A. B. Clarke. VII, 374 pages. 4°. 1974. DM 28,–

Vol. 99: Production Theory. Edited by W. Eichhorn, R. Henn, O. Opitz, and R. W. Shephard. VIII, 386 pages. 4°. 1974. DM 32,–

Vol. 100: B. S. Duran and P. L. Odell, Cluster Analysis. A Survey. VI, 137. 4. 1974. DM 18,–

Vol. 101: W. M. Wonham, Linear Multivariable Control. A Geometric Approach. X, 344 Seiten. 4°. 1974. DM 30,–

Vol. 103: D. E. Boyce, A. Farhi, and R. Weischedel, Optimal Subset Selection. Multible Regression, Interdependence and Optimal Network Algorithms. XIII, 187 pages. 4°. 1974. DM 20,–

Vol. 104: S. Fujino, A Neo-Keynesian Theory of Inflation and Economic Growth. V, 96 pages. 4°. 1974. DM 18,–